Trailing Clouds of Glory

by
Bruce Neath

Our birth is but a sleep and a forgetting:
The soul that rises with us, our life's star,
Hath had elsewhere its setting,
And cometh from afar.
And not in utter nakedness,
But trailing clouds of glory do we come.

William Wordsworth 1770–1850

Spire Publishing
www.spirepublishing.com

First published in Canada 2008 by Spire Publishing.
Spire Publishing is a trademark of Adlibbed Ltd.

A cataloguing record for this book is available from the Library and Archives
Canada. Visit www.collectionscanada.ca/amicus/index-e.html

Designed in Toronto, Canada
by Adlibbed Ltd.
Set in Baskerville and Baskerville Italics.
Printed and bound in the US or the UK
by Lightningsource Ltd.

Cover photograph by Leonard Stace,
thanks to Bill Stace for allowing its use.

ISBN: 1-897312-77-6

Spire Publishing
www.spirepublishing.com

Spire Publishing

www.spirepublishing.com

FOR RICHARD AND JANE

TOM AND LOU

And all my good friends, blessed with
generosity, warm-heartedness, wisdom and
good humour; and tinged, ever so slightly
with madness, born of oil, steam and smoke.

Special thanks to 'Mrs Miggins', who knew
how to work the infernal computer things,
or this would all have remained a sheaf
of semi-drunken ramblings, on scruffy bits of paper.

CHAPTER ONE

Lemon Curd Legacy

The Worcestershire town of Bromsgrove in the 1950's could be found in mirror image in every county of England. It was a market town, when that meant sheep, cows and pigs, and not jeans, C.D's and woolly hats. There were over thirty pubs, four churches and two cinemas. The town had got its priorities right, there was full range to get pissed and thank God for Marilyn Monroe. Schools were public, private, grammar and secondary modern. Everyone in the town was educated, from the sons of gentlefolk to the village idiot. We had several of those, the best known being Dave Rankin, 'Ranty Tanky'. He was a night watchman; he wasn't employed by anyone, he just used to sit on the pavement and watch the night. The pay was poor but it was regular. Everybody knew Dave, he was a gentle, harmless man, and though he thought the constellations were an American pop group, his stellar-inspired wonder never left him until the day he died. I like to think he's up there with the stars now, together with his old bike, which he couldn't ride, 'Dave the cyclist', just visible between Orion and the Plough.

Town worthies not quite bright enough to qualify as idiots, became members of the council, and in Bromsgrove this was also an alias for the 'Court Leet', an archaic body, founded in the middle ages. Bromsgrove's charter, granted in eleven hundred and something, gave it the right to hold a fair, and the town duly celebrated by allowing the pub's to open all day. This was a clever move and was marked by the Court Leet parading through the town visiting every inn for a beer tasting, and each provision shop for an official produce tasting. As the procession staggered up the High Street, led by a scarlet faced bell-ringer, the marchers leant at an ever more acute angle to the ground, finally arriving at the Queens Head, almost on their hands and knees. As the councillors swept past, they were followed by the general populace, who mimicked their governors, but dispensed with the produce tasting part of the ritual. This day of gay abandon continued on into the evening, eventually culminating in the Fair Day Fight.

So never let it be said that Bromsgrove dismissed its heritage. The streets never actually ran with blood, but a fair proportion of the 10,000 population woke up with a black eye and a coconut the next morning. A good time was had by all, with the possible exception of the nursing staff at the Cottage Hospital.

The High Street had proper grocers and butchers shops, four fish and chip salons, a faggot shop and two wet fish merchants. Did anyone ever open a dry fish shop?

The town sat astride the mighty River Spadesbourne, navigable by pooh-sticks right up to the 'Bromsgrove Messenger' offices, and apart from Fair day, order prevailed, everyone was happy with their lot, and life, the universe and everything, moved inexorably on.

Suburbs hadn't been invented and about a half mile from the town centre, in every direction, shops ended and streets of houses began. At the southern end of the town, Highfield Road was just such a street, a card-shuffle mix of Victorian, Edwardian, post war council architecture, notable only for its one Cotswold brick bungalow, built in an apple-cleared orchard, pointing the way forward to a single storey, fruit free future.

This was where my life began.

The street was a riot of children; everyone must have celebrated the war's ending in the same way, we were all the same age, the Midwich Cuckoos, without blond hair.

All the men folk found employment within the boundary of the town. The mighty Garringtons factory employed over 2000 men, and the railway and myriad little factory units, making everything from buttons to badges, provided work for all.

A couple of mills provided jobs for some of the ladies, but in the main the woman's place was still very much in the home.

Domestic creature comforts were still some way off and our home life was typical of many. Upstairs, wire sprung beds and marble topped bedside cabinets were still the order of the day; the ill-named lounge might run to a settee, supposedly filled with horse-hair, but feeling like it contained the rest of him. The 'front room' was the showpiece, where no one was allowed to use the only decent furniture, and the kitchen was

8

more like an ante-room of the inquisition, with its dolly tub and mangle, and sloping deep stone sink with cold and cold running water. The pantry had a stone slab and an air-brick that did duly as a refrigeration unit, and sticky twirling fly-papers served as a mobile insect collection.

The tin bath hung on a nail outside the back door, a constant reminder never to have a bath, and there was no toilet inside the house, until Saturday night, when every room potentially had one.

I once got two black eyes from the heavy, swinging, pendulum, when I drunkenly pissed in the grandfather clock in our hallway. The next morning my mother found time running away, all over the linoleum.

This then was typical England in the early 1950's. We'd won the second great war to end all wars. With outside lavatories prevalent, truly, to the victor, the piles.

Our road climbed steeply up a hill, at the top of which the town ended and the country began. Halfway up the hill was the house of Lou Taylor and her son Bob, who was to become my bosom pal, and later to introduce me to radio comedy, popular music and the lifetime obsession and passion, steam trains and things connected to that 'continuous nervous breakdown'. For whatever reason that I never discovered, Bob was always known to everyone as Spud. He was a year older than me and took me under his wing. I looked upon him as my mentor and he filled my head with sounds and images he conjured up from radio shows, and kept me endlessly amused with whole chunks of comedy routines, that he had learnt by heart. We sat leg swinging on his front garden wall, and sang 'Don't laugh at me' by Norman Wisdom, and 'Because You're Mine' and 'The Lords Prayer' by Mario Lanza. I did of course know that last one, I was a Church of England school boy, and it was the school song.

The age of television was yet to dawn and the only set in the street was owned by the Potter family, and I clearly remember half the street sitting in their lounge, watching the ' Coronation' in 1953, on their telly, housed in a cabinet as big as a wardrobe.

So, what a time in our history this was, we were about to 'never have it so good', hardly anyone had a car or a television set, Christian prayers were top of the pops and being sung by ten year old children in the street, and the whole nation thought Norman Wisdom was bloody funny.

What stark contrast to today in Britain, where it seems we've just had it, car ownership has turned us all into criminals, television is a worldwide, perverted, 'reality' nightmare, even the Archbishop of Canterbury doesn't want us to know the Lords Prayer, and Norman Wisdom's become the patron saint of Albania.

Incidentally, poor old Mario went to Hollywood and gorged himself to death. How different is that; he must have been the first celebrity to die of eating.

Social mobility, or in fact any sort of mobility, was easily defined. We all walked everywhere or rode our bikes. Otherwise the Midland Red Bus company was our transport of delight. Leisure travel was an oxymoron. Going on holiday in a charabanc meant hours, or to Cornwall, days of grinding away at thirty miles an hour, without toilets or air conditioning, precious few comfort stops and definitely uncomfortable seats, down the never ending, packed A38. I think the A stood for Amen.

But for countless thousands of midland families, holidays to the seaside meant this really was the age of the train. During the summer months, Birmingham's New Street and especially Snow Hill stations, packed train loads of bucket and spade laden children and their parents, off to North and mid Wales, the East coast and predominantly the West Country resorts. The term resort and the very existence of towns like Rhyl, Barmouth, Cromer, Paignton and Dawlish, are due entirely to the railways. Because of Spud, I was about to experience the railway phenomenon and witness, in the mid 50's, the busiest time in the history of steam traction in this country.

I know amnesia is a great cure for bad recollections, but to coin an over-used phrase, the nation really did seem to be at ease with itself. The days of raised voices and door slamming in our house were yet to come and no-one I knew was of a worried or tense demeanour. We'd none of us heard of angst, so we couldn't be ridden by it.

Crime appeared to be something only Americans committed on TV and few of us were able to watch it.

Ignorant and boorish behaviour were the province only of the police, publicans and all the staff at Woolworths.

We were the torch-bearers of New Britain, still scrumping apples, riding bikes without bells and ogling 'Health and Efficiency' magazines whilst buying our comics. Happy with our lot, playing ball games in the street until it got dark, paper chasing and hiding in the rabbit warren in Saunders Farm field; dibbing and dobbing in the cubs at First Bromsgrove Scout Group. On reflection I have to say, what a fucking life.

On one such leg-swinging, wall sitting day, mulling over all these exciting recreations, Spud first mentioned the possibility of train spotting down at Bromsgrove station. We cut what must have been the opposite of a dash. Like two ragged-arsed peas in a pod, decked out in grey shirts, knee length grey trousers hitched up with elastic stretch snake-belts, twin colour tank top pullovers, grey socks and black pumps, the whole ensemble looked exactly adequate for a young offenders prison uniform. When all the kids in the street were playing 'tag' in the early evening, an outside observer could be forgiven for thinking a mass midget jail break was in progress.

Adolescence in the street heralded the arrival of acne, rickets, and for some, impetigo. These sufferers stood out of the crowd with their blue faces. It must have been the first time in Britain's history that woad-painted Mercian people went to the corner shop on racing bikes.

It was also the time of the green faced Woodbine smokers, whilst under the scout hut, masturbation was invented.

My friend Eddie at the Church of England School used to get his dick out under the table, during school dinners, especially if we had semolina for pudding. I've never found out the aphrodisiac properties of wheat, but I used to wonder if he carried on in adult life, getting an erection every time dessert was served, you know, like a Manchurian Candidate triggered response. He must have been popular at dinner parties.

Strangely, I cannot remember any pre-planning, but found myself calling for Spud at about seven o'clock one Saturday morning. Waiting in the half light in his mom's little kitchen, smelling of bacon and eggs and damp washing, whilst she proceeded to cut us both two huge door step sandwiches, full to running with lemon curd.

Recipe: Take one jar of lemon curd, one loaf, one packet of butter. Cut loaf into eight slices, spread each slice thickly with butter and curd and pack in grease-proof paper. Throw away empty lemon curd jar and butter packet. Buy new loaf.

Like the two children in the Clark's shoe advert of the time, walking in silhouette with the fingers of dawn radiating out and upwards behind them, we stepped out into the bold unknown.

Actually we trudged the two miles down to the station, Spud carrying the gigantic sandwiches in his dad's khaki 'bait' bag, whilst I did the honours with a huge bottle of dandelion and burdock, (whoever thought of that combination?). I think later on we refilled the bottle with water and used it as a garden roller.

In what seemed no time at all, we were down at the station and found ourselves a pitch on the station wall, straining with anticipation for the first train to arrive from the south. Yellow mouthed and upper-lipped from the fiery 'pop' drink, bearing just a trace of the impetigo blue on the upper cheek bones, we looked like five star generals in Boadicea's army.

Almost silently a 'Jubilee' tip-toed up to the full cross-line signal gantry and eased to a halt, slow hissing and submissive. Way down the line at Newton bridge, two 'jinty' tankers huffed and puffed their way out from the bankers' siding and gently buffered up to the rear of the passenger train. They didn't couple up.

The signal 'peg' came into the off position, the leading engine blew a sharp blast on her whistle, the jinty's answered back and the glorious theatre of Britain's steepest railway bank began to unfold.

With the regulator wide open, a volcanic exhaust roaring high into the sky, the train slammed through the station. The noise was deafening and the platform, and even the station buildings shook. It was a seminal moment, never to be forgotten; I was mesmerised and not a little afraid, as with sound and fury the locomotive thundered past. Blurred images of the seated passengers flew ever faster before my eyes, in the 'blood and custard' rolling stock. The lead engine disappeared in a pall of smoke as she tore under the road bridge at the far end of the station, then began the attack on the daunting bank with a vengeance.

My heart was still in my mouth as the sound rose again to a crescendo, as the two bankers piled on the coals and with full regulator, hammered past me and into the dense smoke cloud. The concrete shook beneath my feet as they were lost from sight in flying, furling clouds of steam and smoke.

I was deaf, my ears ringing, my mouth was dry and I found it impossible to speak. I looked at Spud, like me his face was streaked with watery coal dust, a rainbow of coal and oil formed above our heads, the unique and pungent smell of smoke and hot oil permeated my clothes and my hair. We looked wide-eyed at each other and burst into helpless excited laughter. I was eight years old, I felt vibrantly alive, I'd discovered the Lickey incline.

CHAPTER TWO

Blinkers in the Tunnel

Food rationing officially ended in Britain. For the first time since the war ended, most Britons had the chance to eat not only the feet, tails and stomach plumbing of most animals, but the meaty bits in between as well.

Roger Bannister ran the mile faster than Lou Taylor could butter four lemon curd sandwiches, and there was an eclipse of the sun. The Americans exploded their hydrogen bomb at Bikini, (U.S. foreign policy going tits-up even then), and the sun shone on Bromsgrove station, also a rainless zone, every single day of the summer school holidays.

Spud and I existed on a diet of Wagon Wheels, lemon curd, ice-lollies shaped like Mickey Mouse, Tizer and euphoria.

We plagued the station waiting rooms, exasperated the porters, drove the signalman in the box on the platform to distraction, and generally grew into our new roles as train-spotters. We skipped down the line to Newton bridge, helped the crews to water and coal the bunkers, and were repaid with visits to the footplate on all the 'jintys' and even the great 'Big Bertha', 58100. She was huge and built purposely for her life-time on the Lickey. When she was withdrawn and scrapped in Derby in 1956, the sadness amongst all the spotters, and indeed all the railwaymen at Bromsgrove, was palpable.

Sitting on the embankment down the line towards Stoke, turning pennies into dustbin lids, as the slow and heavy goods engines passed over the coins we'd placed on the line, we watched a never ending procession of holiday trains, waiting nose to tail, for their turn to assault the incline.

On other days we walked along the line, up the bank itself and took residence at Pikes Pool or maybe Vigo bridge.

All day the endless cavalcade of Holiday specials, returning their passengers from the delights of the West Country, stormed past us, aided and abetted by the tireless bankers and 'Big Bertha' herself. Then they somehow found the 'paths' to rattle back down the bank, between the heavy traffic coming in the other direction and once more return to the never ending duties on the incline. These were the days when enginemen

14

earned their corn and could never be paid enough. The consummate skill that allowed two, three sometimes even four, banking engines to come together with no coupling between them, nor between the train and them, then heave three or four hundred tons of resistance up the unforgiving two miles and detach without pile-driving the whole ensemble through the booking office at Blackwell station, was without parallel on British Railways.

We often finished our day at Blackwell, and as the light faded, the raging locos wrote their story of endeavour with hot coals, burning gases and blazing flames in the glowering night sky. "This majestic roof, fretted with golden fire." Perhaps Hamlet caught the night sleeper to Elsinore.

Then, as the final goods train clanked and juddered her rake of coal wagons over the brow of the hill, cheerful wisp of friendly smoke curling out of the guards van chimney, we walked home behind her, as the train, the trees and finally both of us, were lost in the panoply of the blood reddening night sky.

It was during such a night walk back home, with thoughts and chattering about what we'd 'copped' during the day, how splendid 'Leander' looked on the 'Devonian', whether Colin Berwick had been to Fudge Junction (main station on the bullshitters rail network), and how Maureen Alloys had lifted her skirt and showed us her knickers, just because we bought her an ice-lolly, that we made the momentous decision to visit Birmingham New Street the next Saturday. Oh, and to always have ice-lolly money about our persons.

Flushed with excitement, we stood in nervous anticipation as the 7.35 'stopper' wheezed its way into the station. It was a midland compound 4-4-0 with four non-corridor coaches, which had certainly seen better and long ago, younger days. Each compartment had two leather strap drop-windows and was luxuriously appointed with two bench seats, which had been upholstered by a sadist and whose design had been selected by a colour blind graffiti artist. The décor of smoke stained cream and brown was enlivened by sepia vignettes of Midland Spa towns, taken around the turn of the century. This is not meant as a criticism; this was the carriage that was taking us to Brum! God knows what lay in store for us in the big city and we would both have travelled on the day, in a cattle truck.

By wondrous coincidence, Central Trains have continued to make my unspoken thoughts come true and I can now do this whenever I choose, on the Foregate Street to Snow Hill Line. It is not for nothing that this stretch of fantasy railway is known as the 'Dark Side'.

For the first time in both our lives, we found ourselves not watching, but part of the Lickey steam extravaganza. We passed the places where we had sat with our picnics and were soon 'over the top' and wheeling away through leafy Barnt Green, then almost surreptitiously, into the Birmingham suburbs past the seemingly endless mass of the Austin Motor Works and on into dormitory land. With trains passing us with ever more frequency, we plunged into the first of five dark, smoke filled tunnels. With both windows open, the compartment soon became a cinder filled, choking, airless place, until thankfully we burst out into the murky half-light of the carbonic cauldron that was New Street station.

The impact was immediate. I had never seen so many people in one place, going in so many different directions. Where had they all come from? Where were they all going? "The tumult and the shouting dies"; Kipling had never been in this place. It was a controlled and mobile uproar.

We stood in awe on platform twelve, stunned by the sheer bruising, thundering, vocal energy of it all. Two country boys had dropped into the maelstrom of the metropolis. Spud and I stumbled along the platform in a state of catatonia; small dodgem-shaped electric trucks scythed through the milling masses, drawing, swaying, rumbling, grinding and banging, steel-wheeled trolleys, laden with head-high loads of parcels, boxes, newspapers and god know what other merchandise. Snaking along at high speed, with horn blowing and frantic gesticulation from the driver, suddenly to disappear down a dark forbidding tunnel, to reappear, or maybe another of its clan, across the tracks, now miraculously cleared of all its cargo.

Hordes of people storming up the stairways, just as many, elbows flying, tempers rising, forcing their way past them, coming down. Signals clanging, bells ringing, whistles blowing; mail and cases, birds in cages, disgorged from guards vans, force-fed back into others; flags, announcements, comings and goings, trains clanking in, surging out, mayhem, chaos.

I felt the wind ruffle my hair, as a new page in the book of life turned over.

Then where to watch the trains, to best advantage, in all this frantic action? A full exploration of the huge station brought the discovery that it was actually in two distinct parts, separated by a roadway, Queens Drive. Taxis huddled near the central footbridge area, where hordes of passengers continually spilt out into the street. This same footbridge traversed the whole width of both the station areas, and gave access, via stairways, to all the platforms.

By process of elimination, like rabbits bolting down burrows, we visited each platform, until we found the train-spotters nest on platform six. Here indeed were the "tired, poor, huddled masses", but certainly not yearning to breathe free.

Quite to the contrary, we were soon embroiled in the 'New Street quickstep', whereby the station police arrived to remove the whole seething body of coal-dust addicts, only for them, and now us with them, to return minutes later, when the gendarmes had departed. So it continued throughout the day, deportation followed by re-settlement, ad infinitum. No arrests, no cordoning off the crime-scene, no threats, no abuse; we all played the game, coppers versus nutters, same result every Saturday, nil-nil score draw.

Anyway, it kept us all off the streets.

We settled in amongst the New Street faithful, red-engine lovers each and every one, who would have willingly put a blow-torch through anything Great Western. We marvelled at their tales of wondrous sightings under the grimy canopy, mythical intruders from Scotland and East Anglia, once even a mighty 'Coronation', but nobody had actually seen it.

At the end of the platform fence sat a falcon-eyed sentinel who was obviously blessed with night vision.

As the sounds of an approaching train could be heard in the confines of the pitch black, smoke belching tunnel, with uncanny accuracy he would shout out the visitor's identity. Minutes later, when it burst into what passed for the light, in New Street, he was congratulated by the masses. He was almost never wrong.

The highlight of the day was when the shout went up 'Blinkers in the tunnel'! This heralded the arrival of the locomotive with smoke deflectors, a 'Scot', 'Patriot', or even a 'Britannia' pacific. Among the proletariat procession of Birmingham's trains, these were New Street royalty.

At sight of one of these beauties, cacophony reigned supreme. It was like dropping a wasp's nest out of a tree. Shouting, screaming, circling, back-slapping, hand shaking, air-punching, hugging, self congratulatory delirium. It was what we called in today's tight-arsed, controlled and sanitized environment, an interactive moment.

This then was the first of many such days spent with the Brummy boys on platform 6. I met lads who I would see again throughout my life, all over the country, seduced by the lure of steam.

In that dark and dirty, evil-smelling, rickety old cathedral of flaking Victorian brickwork, rusting steel and work-stained broken glass, on the platform altar we all gave thanks for the gift of the steam locomotive.

New lessons were being learnt:

If a burning cinder in your eye was not blinked free in the first ten seconds, you carried it with you all the weekend. Coal dust in your sandwiches didn't taste altogether too bad. Certainly better than mayonnaise. The 'New Street nuisance' was an antiquated loco serving as the station pilot and not the station master, and Birmingham children could see in the dark.

We rattled off home each night and thrummed down the Lickey back to Bromsgrove, tired, dirty and exhilarated. I can't ever remember the two mile walk back home.

The railway world was bigger than we thought, and about to get bigger.

Birmingham New Street Station,
A. W. Flowers

CHAPTER THREE

All things bright and beautiful

Bromsgrove is an old town. Mentioned in the Domesday Book with an ancient charter, it was called, arguments still rage, either Bremesgrove or Boarsgrove. There's a boar on the town's coat of arms, probably because nobody could draw a breme.

It has no fortification, no castle, the Welsh never ventured this far across the Severn, at least not until the Neath's moved in, and the Romans had built one 'cester' just down the road and didn't need another one.

There is a fine Manor house at Grafton and a few tudor buildings in the old High Street, but for the main part it could best be described as a modest town, at least in architectural terms.

At its centre and on the highest ground, stands the Church of St John. It offers commanding views of the town in all directions and from the tower you can see Malvern, Clent, Clee and Bredon hills. This is most apposite, as so were the four houses of the Church of England School, my first school.

Actually, from the tower you can also see the floodlights on West Bromwich Albion's football ground, but I suppose that had too many letters to sew onto the house game's duffel bags.

From the lofty position the churchyard sprinkles its monuments and memorials down three sides of its hill, and almost tips some of them over the buttressed wall of the little school. It was a rite of passage in my schooldays, to be able to run up the buttress and leap over the half-moon brick topped retaining wall and down into the churchyard below.

I was ten years old before I at last managed to do it and avoid being stigmatized for life as a failure.

I returned to the school yard when in my fifties and found that I could stand and place my hand on the walls parapet, but no longer I fear, could I run up the buttress.

On the hillside adjacent to the towns produce and bric-a-brac market, access to the church grounds is by way of a wonderful flight of forty-nine steps, divided into seven sets of seven and accompanying landings. This is ten more steps than John Buchan could manage, and in my football managerial career, became the central feature of my stamina circuit training.

It has to be said, this was the closest to God most of my heathen players ever got and it was certainly noticeable that they recorded faster times on the circuits coming down the stairs, than on those going up.

"As flies to wanton boys, are we to gods,

They kill us for their sport".

Not quite how the lads addressed me after an hour long session, but heart warming nevertheless, to be called a slave-driving bastard. Showed the training was working.

The church was central to my school days, but a welcome addition to the learning process and certainly not dogmatic or propagandist.

Each Friday the whole school trooped up the broad avenue to the west door for the morning service. I remember thinking on those walks, as we strode between the rows of stones of earlier scholars, of all the Bromsgrove children before me and imagined they were passing me on the way down.

St. Johns is an imposing structure, high, wide and handsome, much like the great 'Wool' churches of Norfolk. Our whole school complement was lost inside its commodious nave and our offering up of the mornings hymns made for thin glory indeed. Even so we gave it full throttle and put as much gusto as possible into 'Christian Soldiers', 'All things Bright and Beautiful', 'There is a Green Hill' and all the other ecclesiastical chart-toppers of the time.

Incidentally, until I was about thirty years old, I thought the 'Green Hill' far away hadn't got a city wall, not that it was standing outside one. An embarrassing admission I guess, but anyway, whoever's heard of a girl called 'Be-bop-a-lula'? And we've all sung that with a meaningful look in our eyes.

Every week our repertoire grew and we crashed on gaily, wreaking havoc with the organist's chord progressions. During all those soirees I don't think we ever started, nor certainly finished, at the same time. But occasionally it was a close run thing and the vicar smiled appreciatively. Like the road to heaven itself, not fully tarmaced, but work in progress

Its also interesting to speculate why after all these years, and I never became a regular churchgoer, whenever I hear a hymn playing, be it on

TV or radio, if its one of 'ours', I can still join in and sing all the words. Considering that I sometimes forget some of 'Great Balls of Fire', or 'Jailhouse Rock', it seems St. Johns and the Rev have left their indelible mark.

I had what my teacher called a 'malleable' voice and found myself singing in the church choir, albeit for a very short time. Tony May was the descant and was hallowed and lauded on a Pavarotti-like scale by the girls at School. We all just made up the numbers in his backing vocal group. After about a year the group broke up and so did all our voices.

The Rev. mentioned earlier was Dr. Sheppard, an avuncular, friendly, approachable man, with his shock of white hair, twinkling eyes behind silver-rimmed spectacles and portly build, very much like Father Christmas on his day job. No happy clappy nonsense, nor fire and brimstone sermonising, a man of genuinely gentle and warm demeanour.

I bumped into him a couple of times in the High Street years later, when we were both going about our post school business, and we chatted cheerily and comfortably together as friends. He enquired about my work and general health and always wished me well. He always impressed me as a good man who tried to bring some comfort and genuine care to a parish of working class people, most of whom faced a lifetime of hard and mostly unrewarding toil until their old age. Respect and responsibility were no 'buzz' words in the 50's, but badges to be earned and donated in magnanimity. The Rev. Sheppard sent all his parishioners out into the sunshine of St. Johns hill, with a little more dignity and a finer feeling of their place in the world.

I was much saddened, when later in life, I learned of his death. St. Johns and Bromsgrove is the poorer for his going.

Life at school meantime was a wide and varied tapestry. The staff were made up of the usual mix, nervous novices, fun loving thirty somethings, tweedy dowagers and a couple of dodderers, and a sex symbol, and that was just the male teachers. Not really, although the ladies outnumbered the men by, I think about eight to two. All of these good people were presided over by our indomitable headmistress, Fanny Scale.

Fanny rode to school each day on her bicycle and was so petite, she needed a step ladder to dismount. But god did she pack some zest into that small frame. The woman was a human dynamo, she organised everything at the C. of E. Everyone reported to her, nothing happened without her. The staff stood to attention when she did her classroom inspections (every day), she organised the time-table, the games periods, school outings, the school football XI, sports day and all the church services. I was terrified of her, so were the rest of the pupils and the staff.

One day three of us were caught trespassing in the Council House gardens. Next day we were summoned to Fanny's office. We were dressed down, up, and down again. 'Don't you ever make me eat humble pie again', she said, she was so proud of her school, and though we didn't know it, of all of us as well. We were all mortified that we had let her down, we never did so again.

On the last day of school, before we all left for the big wide world of secondary education, she called me into her office, as I was changing over classrooms. 'I know you're interested in trains, please take these'. She gave me four beautifully illustrated little train books. I've sifted through a mountain of rail memorabilia since that day, but never again seen any of those little books. I have them still.

Monday was dancing class. Being of shy and embarrassed nature until well into my fifties, I used to dread the day. We filed upstairs to the Hall, pausing in the cloakroom to change into our black dancing pumps. Then as Miss Beech, the demon piano player, warmed up with a few arpeggios and exhortations to 'come onto the floor, quickly now', the ordeal began. 'Pair up, pair up, come on Bruce, can't you see Anne is just dying to dance with you'. She might have been, but I was just dying.

Then 'con brio'; 'Roger De Coverly' at eighty miles an hour. Miss Beech used to play the piano like Fats Waller, leaning back then lurching forward to attack the keyboard, head rocking all the while. Power was her game, power and fortissimo. But I have to say she didn't smoke a cigar.

The lesson wore on, Anne and I perspired freely, I gave her more bruises than a wife-beater and set up her chiropodist for life. Miss Beech thundered on, massacring more family favourites from the nineteenth century song book. She would never have been out of work today in a drum and bass band.

Then, with a final flourish, it was over. 'Well done class, I think you're starting to get it'.

Anne would say she'd see me next week and kiss me. I'd glow like a red traffic light all afternoon.

Wednesday was singing class. Not quite so high on the richter scale of terror as the dancing class, but a pretty competitive second place for me. This was mainly because the girls were always the best singers and tended to monopolise the lesson. Also they came dressed in all their finery. Best dresses, pretty shoes, bows in the hair, shining faces, wondrously beautiful.

The boys came dressed in amazement.

Usually the lesson opened with both boys and girls singing counterpoint, and the girls were always more at ease with the harmony than we were. I suppose it's more difficult to concentrate on the melody line when you're drooling.

Later the girls would split into small groups, trio's and even duo's. The most hypnotic of these were the Waldren twins. They were perfect. Linking arms, gently swaying with the music at the beginning. They were identical and as we stood listening and looking at them, the whole assembled class began to sway with them. They moved together ever more as the song continued, it was like an hallucinatory experience, a roomful of intoxicated people moving as one.

I suppose the Liverpool Kop singing 'You'll never walk alone' might run it a close second.

Whenever I drive or walk past the school, now a dull office, full of clicking, tapping, typing, battery drones, I still hear the swell of children's voices and 'Annie Laurie' and 'Sweet Lass of Richmond Hill' rising from the upstairs hall.

An episode has flashed through my memory, that perhaps has no right to sit beside such glowing testaments, but it was such a stunning sight. A lad called Roy Emus could direct his urine, under pressure, over the connecting wall of the boys and girls lavatories, almost at will. To see a perfect parabola of piss, passing through a renal rainbow, was one of the wonders of my childhood. It's also artistically, acceptable alliteration.

I wonder if he became a fire-fighter in adult life.

There were never any problems with children in the classrooms that I can recall, if you discount Margaret Wilde wetting herself during almost

24

every lesson. The poor girl obviously had a weak bladder and was just unable to control herself. The school's answer to this was to tie a coloured ribbon to her chair, so that no-one else inadvertently used it.

How traumatic this was to Margaret, or 'Pisser Wilde' as she was universally known, I can never know. What she, and adult life, held in store for each other, I shudder to think. Junior schools in the 50's just got on with the educating job, and dealt with the side issues in an uncompromising manner. Political correctness then meant doffing your cap when the local M.P. passed by in his Daimler.

But all of this changed when break-time came along at 11.00am and the school gang's assembled. The larger and more aggressive of Bromsgrove's primary education system, or 'rough little bastards' as Mr. Beswick so graphically described them, spent all this session recruiting traumatised new members. Fully versed even at this tender age, in the art of child terror, the gang leaders would beat the afternoon game plan into the rookies and one last minute drill would ensure that everyone knew his place and his job, come the afternoon break.

Three o'clock brought the hoodlum's show of strength. The school could be completely circumnavigated by means of an alley that connected the two ends of the three-sided playground. No architect in his nightmares could have possibly imagined the singular use this feature played host to, day after day.

After lining up in order of seniority, size, ugliness and sheer brutal capability, the two gangs set off from different ends of the school, in different directions and began roaring round the building. They formed two fearsome cavalcades of screaming, whooping, Indian war cry imitating raggedy ruffians, circling the school, passing each other at speed, but never colliding. Each was led by a blazing eyed fanatic who carried the gang's colours. This was usually a handkerchief, painted during the art lesson, attached to a broom handle and held above the head, pointing forward like a standard on the prow of a ship.

The two linear mobs continued to orbit the school until fatigue, or the school bell, called a halt to the proceedings.

"I'll put a girdle round about the earth in forty minutes".

The future electorate of Bromsgrove put several round their school if fifteen.

The greatest of these apache impersonators was Bob Banner, who was my friend at school and stayed a friend through teenagery, young thuggery and middle-aged debauchery. He became a member of the Oddfellows, a snooker ace, legendary drinker, fearless footballer, nightclub bouncer, woman charmer, and sometime furniture van driver for me, when I ran dad's business.

Now that's what I call putting your early education to full and proper use.

John Sweeney was a singular chap. He was Irish, shy, read a lot and collected farm yard models. (I mean models of pigs, cows, sheep etc., not bikini-clad lovelies reclining on tractors). He kept himself very much to himself and was naturally a target for 'bash him up in the playground' games.

For what was the only time in my life, I allowed someone to talk me into picking a fight. I've managed since then to get into a few without any help whatsoever.

I picked on John one break time, although I quite liked him. I wanted to get the deed done quickly for my heart wasn't really in it. I took a swing and hit him in the face. He didn't flinch. I hit him again and he flinched, but he complemented the flinch with a perfect straight jab that split my nose open. I bled like one of his farmyard pigs. As I bowed my head in shock and disbelief, he grabbed my hair and walked away with half my scalp.

Blinded and half bald, unable to breathe through my nose and choking on my own blood, my sponsors held up my arm and hailed me as the winner. Thank fuck he didn't beat me, I thought to myself. That night I made two decisions, I'd never pick another fight with a quiet Irishman and I'd take up boxing.

Mr. Beswick had boxed in the army and was delighted to pass on his knowledge of the noble art of self-defence. I could have used some of this before the 'Sweeney incident' I mused, but better late than thrashed again. He set up a ring in the dancing/singing hall and I put on my first pair of boxing gloves. They had seen much better days. They were old, soft and very big, filled with enough horse hair to stuff a three-seater settee. If you had them laced up for you in the classroom and held your arms down at your sides, you couldn't get through the door.

My pal Bob Bagshaw sparred with me under Mr. Beswick's guidance and he taught us how to balance ourselves, basic footwork, ducking and weaving and covering up against attack. We were learning fast and enjoying it. We could cross, straight jab, cover up, counter and spit into the bowl in the second's corner, without getting spittle all over the canvas.

Mr. Beswick decided it was time Bob and I put on an exhibition bout for the school. We were great rivals at everything. He was a yard faster than me over the hundred yards, twenty yards ahead at the end of the cross country, just had the edge on me with ball control in football, and had a prettier sister. I knew this time I would beat him. I was knocked out for the first time in my life in the third round. Everyone in the school had seen the punch coming, except me. Lying down quietly on the canvas, stars in my eyes, my head spinning, not knowing who I was; perfect training for the 'top of the town Pub runs', to come in a few short years time.

I did a little boxing as a 'boy weight' at the Austin British Legion club, but I didn't have the aptitude. I couldn't stop myself reverting to the southpaw stance, even during the course of a bout, it was not a good tactical move. Mr. Beswick had told me, unless I could master the orthodox stance, a good counter puncher would rip my left ear off. I was talking to him years later over a pint and he asked me how the boxing had gone on. I said 'you what?'.

So I was leaving school three months before my 12th birthday, with a pretty impressive looking C.V., even at that tender age. That is if anyone was looking for a singing, dancing, punch drunk, wig-wearing member of the mafia.

Just in case anyone who was there ever reads this, my favourite people in 1955 were, in no particular order, Marilyn Monroe, Rocky Marciano, Susan Hicks, Miss Clayson (the sex symbol), Bob Bagshaw, Elvis Presley and the Platters.

CHAPTER FOUR

Clangers

In Woody Allen's film 'All you ever wanted to know about sex.....' he had a machine called the Orgasmatron. It was about the size of a telephone box, but it must have contained more than a 'phone and a directory. Woody went in, then came out of it after a few minutes, looking deliriously happy and extremely satisfied. Lets admit it, British Telecom just doesn't have that effect on people.

When I was thirteen I found exactly such a conjurers box that used to send me out into the real world in a similar condition. It was a transport café on Station Approach in Tamworth.

When I say transport café, I really mean garden shed, for that indeed was the architectural statement that it made. But once inside, the place was surely the 'stately pleasure dome decreed'. Kubla Khan Builders Merchants must have had a branch in Tamworth, before Buildbase bought them out.

Spud and I had discovered Tamworth, courtesy of the 'Platform Six' gang and found our train from New Street full of wide-eyed believers on their way to Staffordshire's mecca. Listening to the stirring tales of what we were about to see and what had already been seen, I was so excited I nearly bought a ticket. At this point I have to make a sad and embarrassing admission. Both Spud and myself had been talked in to 'bunking' the fare by a silver-tongued cove, with a more than passing resemblance, both in dress and demeanour, to the Artful Dodger. He was one of a group of likely lads who grew up to be the 'neverers', who boldly went all over the rail network in the pursuit of steam, and whose proud boast was that they never paid the ticket price.

In its great and legendary heyday in the late 50's and early 60's Tamworth was a magnet for all Midlands rail enthusiasts. Rugby and Lichfield Trent Valley drew their crowds, but this was the place to be. The station had high and low level platforms, which crossed at 90 degrees. In the summer months huge crowds gathered in 'the field' just beyond the platform ends, on the south side of the West Coast main line. The high level ran across the centre of the lower station and carried the Bristol to

Derby main line. Trains on this embankment could be seen approaching from a considerable distance in both directions, whilst below, a long straight heralded approaching north-bound trains, and the London bound expresses burst excitingly from the confines of the station. On the West Coast line a steady stream of express trains ran at very high speed past the field and it was unusual to see any freight activity during the Saturday day-time period.

On the top level however, the passenger traffic was sandwiched between a seemingly endless procession of heavy coal trains, black exhausts blasting vertically to the heavens as they strove to keep the road clear for the faster traffic. A constant blanket of conversation across the field, trains appearing, exhausts drumming, from one, two, sometimes all four directions at once.

To paraphrase Captain Strahan, when asked what his images of the war were, "Oh my dear fellow, the noise, ... and the people".

Yet even here, there came a period of the day, the 'dud hour', when groups of spotters ambled off the field, through a tunnel under the High level, to sample the delights of the café.

I never managed to work it out, but the place was never overcrowded, even though at some point during the day, everyone in the field came in for food, a drink and ten pence on the Jukebox. Just how this tiny shack managed to feed this tumultuous mob, and where they kept all the stock, remains a mystery to this day. The guv'nor was a swarthy, bearded man, perhaps he'd done an earlier gig in another life, with loaves and fishes.

'A la carte' was bacon or sausage and tomato sandwiches, with tea, tizer or expresso coffee. I have to say I've rifled through a few decent restaurants and eaten some pretty exotic tucker in my time, but never have I enjoyed anything more than the café menu. 'Swarthy man' was a genius on a primus and had several hundred addicts to prove it.

Whoever designed the shed was obviously a rail-fan. Whether you sat or stood, windows on the embankment side and another behind the counter, gave perfect sight-lines of both main line tracks. Everything began to shake when a train approached, so there was never a chance of missing a 'cop'.

Music was taking over my soul and the Jukebox was a cornucopia of unforgettable, classic rock and roll. Elvis, like the café, was 'All shook up', Little Richard 'kept a knocking', The Everlys sang 'Bye Bye Love', Frankie Lymon was a 'Juvenile Delinquent', Buddy Holly said 'That'll be the Day' and Paul Anka made a million by saying 'O' at least twelve times to 'Diana'.

There were always black and white postcards of trains passing through Tamworth on sale in the café. I never found out who the photographer was. Also available were copies of the wonderful shot of Marilyn Monroe in her white dress, standing over the hot air grating. The guvnor knew his business and understood his customer's requirements. I always spent every halfpenny I possessed in the Café and came out with half a dozen action-shots on the main line and a Marilyn. He played us all like Stradivarius violins and we loved every minute of the concert.

I reckon he was in league with the devil.

Whilst watching a documentary about the Wildebeest migration across the Masai Mara, it occurred to me how like the 'Tamworth Field Experience' it was. There was the herd, snorting comfortably and casually grazing, when suddenly, as though someone had fired a starting pistol, they all upped sticks, and hooves and horns flying, made a headlong dash for the Mara River.

In our case, a drowsy, bee-humming, summer afternoon, lying on the grass, chewing on our sandwiches, ingesting the dreaded Tizer, chatting over trains, life, the universe and everything, then up goes a cry, 'Main' or 'Clangers'. These were the names given to the Signals on the West Coast main line, denoting northbound and southbound trains. On hearing this clarion call, even if in mid bite, swig or chat, everybody rose from their dormitory areas and strode purposefully to the high fence at line-side.

If coming from the south, a blob of white against the skyline, growing to a billowing cloud, steel on steel, click-clacking, ever louder, a growing roar and then, in swirling, shaking, blinding thunder, the train tore past and was lost in Tamworth's brick and timber sanctuary. Then echoes, as she drifted on along the Trent Valley and in a very few seconds, all sounds were swallowed up in bee and bird song, and she was gone, away to Stafford and the north.

The southbound trains gave much less notice, unseen beyond the station, and approaching through a cutting, the sound and fury was upon the field, almost in an instant. Only the Stanier pacifics, particularly the Duchesses, gave unique tidings of their approach. Caught for only a few seconds between the high-sided banks north of the station, the staccato beat of four cylinders, with their unique drumming sound, 'dum dum dum dum', was known to all, and remains clear in my mind and memory.

With each passing, bedlam ruled, as emotions ran riot. Elation, disappointment, 'cop' or 'scrap it!' cheers, boo's, manic joy or boredom. I still remember one guy who 'copped' his last Patriot, 'Illustrious'. He threw his arms, books, pens and anything else not bolted down, into the air, and spun round and round like a dervish, screaming out the engine's name. Red-faced and ranting, he eventually sank to the floor. I thought he was having an epileptic fit. But he was a train-spotter; it was just another symptom of the 'continuous nervous breakdown', as a friend of mine so succinctly put it.

Time has moved on: the field is now a chalet park, the station is corporate ghastly and the front layout has laid waste the cobbled approach road, and of course, the café. I've passed through the station since, with steam, on several occasions and once, I went back to visit the site on foot. It was still possible to walk down by the fence and even under the main line, alongside the now stagnant and evil-smelling River Anker. I walked slowly back and looked up to the high level on the embankment, now so overgrown, that full size trees obscured the views in both directions.

It was all overwhelmingly depressing.

As I made up my mind to depart and never to come back, a Pendolino hissed through the station and clattered off down to London. I clutched the same fence that I'd held and peered through, nearly fifty years ago. For a moment I heard again the ghosts of 1957, the Tamworth Boys; the Pendolino was a 'Duchess', the ground shook, and in the distance, the smell of sausage and tomato wafted through the air, carrying an old refrain from Buddy Holly, "Well, that'll be the day, when you say goodbye…..".

31

CHAPTER FIVE

Football by Association

Bromsgrove Rovers v Lye Town; a night match at the Victoria ground, rain slanting across the pitch and right through most of the people standing in the Stourbridge Road corner. Picking out faces as the crowd sauntered in, shapes caught in the old floodlights that nearly reached the ground.

An intermingling cocktail of football smells emanated from the clubhouse/dressing room complex; Linament, Bovril and Bank's beer assaulted the senses.

With a series of club stewards, not too particular about their cellar-work, and decidedly lax in the pipe-cleaning department, it was often a decent option to drink the linament and have a rub down with the Banks's.

Nobody ever drank the Bovril. When the Russian team Moscow Spartak came over to play the Wolves in 1954, I think they took some Bovril back with them and used it as fuel to kick-start their space rocket programme. It was so hot, it was impossible to hold the cup, even after the game had finished. I reckon some of the fans used to creep back into the ground the next morning and have it with a slice or two of toast, for their breakfast.

The teams warmed up, or because of the lack of decent lighting, ran into each other, the goal posts, and members of the crowd. Stray dogs on the pitch, especially if white, were often blasted into the back of the net during the kick-about.

Peering over match-lit programmes, held in mittened hands, we desperately strained our eyes to determine the playing line-up; this was never easy, even in daylight, in the half dark it was impossible, due to the fact that the A4 folded sheet was printed in the Rovers' colours, green letters on a white background. It could only have been worse had the team played in a red and orange ensemble. Consequently, we all waited eagerly for the tannoy system to crackle into life, and hoped to God the announcer hadn't tried to drink his Bovril. This then, should have been the antidote to dreadfully colour-uncoordinated printing, but sadly this was not to be, as this being the late fifties, the committee had discovered rock n' roll. Or, to be more precise, they'd discovered Bill Hayley's

'Rock around the Clock', and must have all fallen hopelessly in love with it, as it remained the only record played in the ground for at least five years.

The result of this amorous folly was twofold, one, that it was played whilst the teams were being introduced, and two, that the needle of the gramophone had last been sharp around V.E. day. It was cacophony layered upon fiasco. "One, two, three o'clock, (scratch, scratch) 'In goal, Skit', "four o'clock rock" (scratch, scratch) 'at left back Joe Wainwright', "five, six, seven o'clock" (scratch, scratch) 'at right back Nodder Oldenhurst' (scratch, scratch), and on it went, sometimes requiring two renditions, in order to get through both teams. So before the match, due to appalling acoustics, we couldn't hear who was playing, whilst after the kick-off, owing to totally inadequate flood-lighting, we couldn't see who was playing.

In those far off days, in the old West Midlands league, both teams were civilly applauded onto the field, but, it has to be said, not always so enthusiastically clapped back off it. The standard of football could best be described as hard, committed and enthusiastic, it could perhaps honestly be described as fucking dangerous. For a forward to turn out without two-inch thick shin-guards was tantamount to inviting amputation of the leg below the knee. Any full back not nicknamed 'chopper' or 'hocker' was universally condemned by the fans as being homosexual, and any forward not bow-legged and riddled with arthritis before he was twenty five, was plainly a public school waster, his time better spent playing for the rugger side at Finstall Park.

The effort put into the ninety minutes was beyond reproach, and considering the lads all trained on Banks's Mild and Players Navy Cut cigarettes, something not far short of miraculous. Real flair or ability however, stood out like a rose in chaff and any new player displaying balance, clever footwork and ball control, was soon brought down to the required skill level.

How strange to consider, that nearly half a century later, the same mentality seems to prevail in English football. I remember listening in deep despair to Ron Atkinson, watching Paul Gascoigne weave his magic in the World Cup in 1990. "Look at bloody Gazza, doing bloody fancy tricks, in a World Cup Quarter Final!"

Perhaps overlooking the fact that Brazil had already won the trophy three times, with all eleven players joyously exhibiting their repertoire of just those same wonderful tricks, what a crushing indictment against an English First Division manager to lambaste mercurial talent, and possibly our only hope, in that tournament, of even reaching the final.

Ron would have felt comfortable at the Victoria, watching the boys give it full aggressive, destructive throttle; after all he used to play just like them.

My boyhood friend Ray Suckling and his cousin Fred, used to stand with me and several other hardy souls, on the Stourbridge Road corner. This was on the migration route from the clubhouse, via the north goal stand, to the West stand. On wet evenings, and I can't remember a dry one, the track would soon become a midden.

Sensing the opportunity this presented for fun, the players wasted no chances to slam the ball, with either boot or head, out of play, into the morass.

You could always identify the 'corner flag mob' in the bar afterwards, they were all wearing brown; several of them carried faithful facsimiles of the ball's stitch pattern on their foreheads. Everybody looked like they'd walked through a car wash. That's what support is all about.

The club-house was a monument to bad taste. Originally decorated in the Rovers' colours, green and white, the ravages of time and the supporters, had continued to amend the décor to smokers-cough brown and mushy peas. The blood-shot red and lightning yellow upholstery on the wall benches juxtaposed pleasingly, and the sprinkling of chairs and tables, none of which matched, completed the adventurous ensemble.

All of these pleasing features combined to ensure that on a strictly social level, the Rovers remained streets ahead of all their league rivals.

I visited many of the black country grounds in those days and furniture of any kind was often an optional extra. Wallpaper, or even paint, was considered effete and it was wise to take your own glass to one or two of the darker venues. At Gornal Wood a small firearm, or at least a club, was advisable.

In the 'Rough Guide to West Midlands Football Grounds' the opening chapter began: "As a general rule of thumb, never enter a clubhouse with blood running down the inside of the windows".

Ray Suckling's mom and dad, Jack and Mick, (no, not cartoon characters, his mom's real name was Michelle), were both club stalwarts. In fact, if you'd broken them in half, like sticks of rock, they were green and white all the way through.

They both did the 'hard yards', and operated the tea-hut and the Bovril scalding centre. I admired Jack greatly. I reckon any man who could inflict so much pain on his fellow, and charge him for it, was a bloody genius.

It didn't stop there; they were involved in every aspect of the club, the sort of people who make local football tick; only when they've gone, does it become apparent how much of the fabric of the club they hold together.

When Jack died, the club player of the year trophy was named after him. I was there on the first occasion Ray presented it and I know how justifiably proud he was.

In my youth, the club zenith was the period that Gil Merrick, the ex England goalkeeper, was manager. He was an aloof, and even anti-social man, not given to mixing with the fans in the bar, and maybe not such great shakes as a manager, but God, he brought some starry names to the Victoria ground. The Hellawell brothers from Birmingham City, Dennis Isherwood, Graham Leggatt of Fulham, Norman Deeley of Wolves fame and for me, the finest of them all, Ivor Allchurch, the great Welsh inside forward. While the Rovers never set the league on fire, nor won the championship, the quality of joy in the football was infectious. The crowds increased two-fold, the clubhouse was redecorated, Norman Deeley set an all-comers record in reaching the bar before any other player had got out of the bath and the fans stopped asking Gil whether the Hungarians had really been any good, when we played them at Wembley in 1953.

To cap it all, he brought an all-star XI to the ground for a charity match and a certain S.Matthews played on the right wing. What a night, it even stopped raining. We didn't care that we were standing in a bog, in the dark. We all went the night that Stan played against the Rovers.

"Magni nominis umbra. - The shadow of a mighty name".

CHAPTER SIX

Abeunt Studia in Mores

It was ten to nine on a crisp September morning. I ambled through the gates of Bromsgrove County High School to begin my new chapter of life in secondary education. The headmaster, Mr. Barron, had dropped dead just a few minutes earlier in the staff room. I don't think it was because he knew I was joining the school, but if I'd known then what an omen was, I reckon I would have thought it was an ill one.

All over the playground people gathered in groups to discuss the endless possibilities, was it natural causes, murder most foul, who'd be the beak, now that Barron was gone? We were all summoned to the hall where the deputy head, Mr. Williams, widely known at Bill-will, gravely announced the demise of our head Mr. Barron. He gave no insight into his passing, but he did give us all the day off.

During the summer holiday break, a new hall of prayer had been commissioned, so it was a case of waiting for the white smoke to emanate from the chimney of the pristine chapel. This it duly did and we found the new 'boss' amongst us, in the guise of E.J.S. Kyte, Oxford mathematician and general academic good egg. He was a tall, wide shouldered man, with steel rimmed spectacles fronting sharp blue eyes in a square jawed, high cheek boned face, topped with short, side parted, steel grey hair. He cut an imposing figure as he wafted bat-like, in his gown and mortar board, along the corridors of the school.

During the first few days of his tenure, he personally interviewed all the years' new intake, no mean feat, I thought, and in due course my turn for the audience arrived. I was summoned to his study and waited with some trepidation for the green light to call me in. I entered and found myself peering at him across a large mahogany desk. I say peering, because I had just been fitted with my first pair of National Health Service spectacles. They were a garish circular lensed, mottle brown rimmed, wire ear-pieced creation, obviously invented by a sadist, who I imagine, must have lurked outside school playgrounds, watching the kids who wore these hideous contraptions being beaten up every day. They didn't come with a health warning, but a notice to hang around your neck, saying 'I'm a complete nerd, please punch me in the face, I deserve it'.

'Ah, Neath' he said, 'I see you are blossoming out into eye glasses'. This opening gambit determined that I would loathe Kyte for ever and never wear the glasses again in school. My high school life of stumbling semi blindness had begun.

Oddly my eyesight had deteriorated from perfect to 'where are you', between the ages of 10 and 11. The optician told me that it was quite a common occurrence, but then again he also asked me if I could see the sun without the glasses, and when I said that I could, he laughingly said 'Well that's 84 million miles away, how far do you want to see?'. I opined that a doctor with that sense of humour was capable of telling you anything.

The first term began in a temporary building known as the 'A hut'. I use the term 'temporary' loosely, as the shed had obviously been in use for at least twenty years, according to the dated, lust-based graffiti carved into its timbers.

The colourful parade of post-war, fading academics otherwise known as the teaching staff began through class 1-3, the system being based on the year number and then divided into three groups, depending on the names initial. Thus everyone from Albert Nasty to Norman Zambezi was in my class. The staff were an amalgam of the Aristocratic, the autocratic and the arthritic. Some were plainly awaiting death's last caress and some, including the younger ones, were clearly deranged. It was indeed a brave new world, with people like this in it.

The day was divided into eight periods, five before lunch and three afterwards. Monday, period one was Latin and brought our first encounter with Mr. Jones, or 'Gobbo' as he was universally known. He fitted effortlessly into the deranged category. His tutorial style could be best described as manic dynamic. Our translations of all things archaic were accompanied by classroom enactments, thus bringing to Worcestershire life every facet of civilization in Roman and Greek early history. I think his finest hour saw him create two battleships from the classic period, of the Bireme configuration. This consisted of two rows of desks, with secondary rows placed upon them. We then manned the oars, actually broomsticks and three foot rulers, and proceeded to row together up the classroom, with Gobbo beating time with a tin tray. This could well be the only time the Greek navy went to war in a prefab. Unconventional his methods may have been, but these animated tableaux ensured that at least some of the ancient language was assimilated and was a far cry from the learn by rote of porto portas portat.

It is heart warming to record that I gained a respectable pass mark in the subject in my first year. It turned out to be the high point of my Latin achievement and the road from then on was sadly all down hill.

First form English was the domain of Beatrice Clegg, 'Aunty Beatty'. She used to think and dream in colour. She told us so. It was of no apparent use in her dress sense. 'Dress Co-ordination' to Beatty meant wearing no more than seven different colours at once, including two different ones for her knee socks. She was a delightful, absent minded old dear, and once, without looking, pulled a rubber snake out of her desk drawer, and attempted to use it to chalk the blackboard. Only midway through the sentence did she realise her chalk stick was an asp, and with a piercing scream, flung it from her and ran sobbing from the room. I have to say, although the class fell about laughing, I soon found myself feeling ashamed of the whole episode, and am only sorry that I didn't tell her so. For several weeks she refused to teach us and only relented when a visit from the 'boss' confirmed that a whacking would be forthcoming, would any further nonsense take place. It was a punishment that I, and a few of my pals, was to become intimately acquainted with in the not too distant future.

French was the remit of Judith Hubbard, a petite and vivacious lady, whose French pronunciation caused me to drift into a reverie even at that tender first-year age. The school rumour machine had it on good authority that four members of the upper sixth had made love to her in the science lab one evening. No that's what I call French chemistry, and perhaps that's why they were known as the upper sixth. Whether it happened I don't know, but I certainly dreamt that it happened with me and so did most blokes in the class, even the whole school. She left the school at the end of the year, and although I had a good exam result in year one, I decided to abandon the subject in the second year in her honour. 'Bonjour Bruce' would never sound the same coming from someone else's mouth.

Music was beginning to interest me, and Tennessee Ernie Ford's '16 tons' and Lou Bush's 'Zambesi' were the late summer chart toppers. Elvis and his 'Heartbreak Hotel' were just around the corner and about to change the world of 'pop' forever.

Then I found out that Miss Longmuir and Miss Scatchard were lesbians. Sometime later I found out what lesbians were. Individually they were Art and History, but god only knew in those innocent years, what they were together. It was only in year three when I discovered two girls from my form playing 'Nurses and nurses' in the corner of the sports field, that the penny, and the knickers, dropped.

It would be unkind to say Miss Longmuir was ugly, but lord knows she was plain. However she brought a fresh and vital enthusiasm to the Art classes and I learnt a great deal from her. I bet Miss Scatchard did as well. Her History lessons were solid and dependable, just like she was, the two of them bore out the old adage that opposites attract. It was forever disconcerting though to sit and wonder at each lesson, what they had been doing to each other the night before. Maybe Jean Longmuir painted great dates in British history all over Miss Scatchard's stomach and thighs. They only taught the first formers, so mercifully those thoughts slipped from my mind when the second year began.

Mr. Hobbs taught Biology, and bearing in mind my new found preoccupation with the human body, it is sad to relate that I failed to bring this zest to the life study of rats, mice, amoebas, fish and pigeons. The practical work which involved dissecting the above species completely failed to stimulate me. However I did become an expert zoological artist, thanks to Miss Longmuir and Maud Jepson. 'Maud' was the iconic text book that contained all the drawings of the animal kingdom, each one pinpointing internal organs and other intriguing features.

Mr. Hobbs used these drawings as a form of 'lines' for poor work results or bad classroom behaviour. Thus on a sliding scale of scholastic crime, he would issue you 5 trout, 6 pigeons, 7 rats etc. to be completed for next morning. Although adept at constructing 'five pen' holders to speed the line producing process, there was no way this could be improvised to draw the sketches, and I often beavered away late into the night to complete my compositions. To this day I can knock up a fairly accurate rat, trout or pigeon, complete with cloaca, dorsal fin, or primary feathers, where applicable.

Mr. Williams ploughed on at school into what appeared to be his dotage and with coloured string tied round almost every finger, each one representing some long forgotten vital task, he turned amnesia into an Olympic event. He was so absent minded, I'm sure he'd even forgotten where he'd left that.

Ken Proctor, the soft spoken senior History master, could not conceal his contempt for the working class children and the only surprise was, that he didn't have a playground hanging from the netball gantry each break time.

Percy Holbrook was our woodwork teacher and bloody good he was too. I do believe he even made his own hockey stick, for he played the sport at a pretty good level, for Cannock in the national first division. My skills in this department left much to be desired and my final project in year three, which was marked for examination purposes, was to be a folding coffee table. This it managed to do admirably, but unfortunately I couldn't make the thing stand up. Percy pointed out that a coffee tray was absolutely useless and marked me 5% and described it thus; 'flimsy, feeble effort'. When he discovered I'd procured enough timber to build a life-size replica of Noah's Ark, the table assumed another purpose, as he set about flattening my arse with it.

I didn't progress in the subject into year four, but I did get my own back on him for the coffee-table thrashing, when the school first XI at football took on the staff, in the end of term hockey match. Percy scored several times and the staff won handsomely, but I did manage to leave the Slazenger logo on my stick on both his ankles.

Ernie French was my maths teacher and was quick to spot that I couldn't see his diagrams on the blackboard, as I sat at the back of class, hoping he wouldn't notice me. In what I first thought was a humiliation in front of the class, he made me attend with him at the blackboard and twang a length of chalked string to create the geometrical shapes during the lesson. However, I later realised that he was making certain that I knew what was going on and to prove his point. I gained my only maths pass mark, during his tuition year. The whole class looked forward to the lessons and Ernie and I began to work as a comedy double act. Just think if my name had been Eric …….. So I became something of a geometric celebrity and my reputation as a joker began to grow. I held court at break-times, I was a legend in my own lunchtime. Years later working for my dad in the removals business, I took Ernie and his belonging down to Somerset, where he retired. We talked about schooldays and I thanked him for all his help. My maths have never been a strong point, but whatever character I have now, a part of it was honed and strengthened by Ernie French.

Games were the province of John Scollen, Peter Leyton and the multi talented George Mills. Scollen was a bully and mercilessly tracked the poor performers, often physically attacking them, and forever shouting and screaming abuse. He turned some of the kids, especially the fat boys, into basket cases, I remember them sweating, crying and being sick, just because the games period was approaching.

Revenge was sweet, and almost terminal, when, during a gymnasium class, our team dropped the horizontal bar on Scollens head, as we all prepared the equipment for circuit training. He went down like a pole-axed animal, we thought we'd killed the sadistic bastard, and the whole class shouted 'Yes!' and clapped. Honestly. He did survive however and shortly afterwards he left the school, probably to become a prison warder, or some other appointment where his skills would be appreciated.

Pete Leyton took the football games and also coached the school elevens from under-15 upwards. He played for Bishop Auckland and had won an Amateur Cup winners medal with them. 'Bishops' were a great force in the amateur game in those days together, coincidentally, with other north eastern sides like Crook Town and Tow Law. The Newcastle Brown must have had a secret ingredient in that era. Pete was a flair player and urged all his teams to express themselves. Attack was everything, as indeed it was with 'Bishops' themselves. Score more goals than the other side, that was the plan, he said, and our gifted players revelled in his training sessions. I was lucky enough to play for the school with some real talent, and Pete's team embarked on a golden era during his tenure. We played in a loosely structured league against South Birmingham and black country grammar schools, including Oldbury Grammar, which had earlier produced Duncan Edwards. I know time gilds the memory, but I can't remember losing many games.

Then there was George Mills. George rolled up the school drive every morning in a golden yellow Triumph Mayflower coupe. He left the hood open and parked wherever the fancy took him. No one ever asked him to move it.

His first love was cricket and he was still playing for Stourbridge in the Midland league. He'd taken his coaching exam and gained an MCC coaching badge. George was always on your side if you showed any talent for the game, and I was quite a tidy fast bowler. My batting, due to my dire eyesight, was of the 'six or out' variety. He said there were three sorts of fast bowler, 'quick', 'very quick' and 'demon'. I was approaching very quick, so I did enjoy rattling the woodwork on match days. However woe betide anyone who didn't take the game seriously. I once threw a hissy fit out on the square, during practise and threw my bat onto the wicket. He gave me five nights detention and made me weed the match wicket with a nail file. By the end of the week I knew every blade of grass by name. 'This is a gentleman's game, conduct yourself properly'. No more hissing or fitting for me. George occasionally weighed in with the football XI when Pete was unavailable and after one gruelling match with, I think King Edwards, we managed to win it with the last kick of the match. George went straight to our captain in the changing room, 'Well done Cottrill, you little bastard'. Slow to divide and swift to bless, just like the old hymn. I'm also reminded that although the girls' were called by their Christian names, it was always surnames for the boys. I still think of all my school mates by surname and have to check myself when meeting new people, even to this day, and not to use the same handle.

Away from these outside pursuits George became my English teacher in forms 4 and 5, and I was playing occasional Sunday cricket for Hanbury and then Avoncroft, where I'd often bump into George at the 'Grasshopper' after the match. He was more concerned over my ignorance regarding decent beer, than the fact that I was only fifteen years old, but nobody would ever turn an Avoncroft cricketer out of the pub, especially if he'd scored a few runs, or taken a wicket or two. It was here on sunny Sunday afternoons that George discussed Tom Graveney and Brian Statham, Tom Finney and Alfredo De Stefano, Shakespeare and Keats, real ale and malt whiskey. After one Eurovision song contest, then in its infancy, he gave me detailed instructions on how to talk to

Parisian ladies, and not get knifed in the bar, for any lack of finesse or improper suggestions.

I also used to run into him at Bromsgrove Rovers, when George and his schoolmaster mate 'killer' Drury, used to stand on the terrace behind the town goal.

George Mills taught me to love the English language and opened the doors of my imagination to appreciate skill and artistry in all facets of life.

'Abeunt Studia in Mores', the school motto; 'study forms character'. More than anyone else, George was responsible for moulding the form of my character in the classroom and on the playing fields of Bromsgrove County High School.

The Devil's Music arrives in Worcestershire (1958)

It was a violent strumming, day dream numbing,
Exhilarating, syncopating second coming.
Little Richard, Jerry Lee and Elvis rocking,
The Law, the Government and Parents knocking,
It was cosmic, seismic, fucking shocking.
It was thunderous, wondrous, you were pissed, bed wetting;
Wanking in your bedroom passed for heavy petting.
Enlightening, frightening, a new life dawning,
Crystals of beer up your nose in the morning.
Cousin John, the Ark Royal, on a shore-leave outing,
Always finished up with the old man shouting.
Wasted on the door step, covered in muck,
Cos earlier you'd crawled down the back-street brook.
Staggering, lurching, brick-wall glancing,
It was Bromsgrove late night shadow dancing.
Just like bopping in the world cup finals,
But your nose keeps bleeding in the pub urinals.
Lying in the gutter watching Halley's comet,
Wondering why your chips always smelt like vomit.
Half-moon pockets, drain pipes, winkle-pickers,
A camouflage to get you into some girl's knickers,
Lusting, dribbling, heavy breathing.
Mackie 'black and tans' and testosterone seething,
Double vision and a stomach cramp,
Bare arse burning on electric lamp;
Teenage love to the sounds of Pat Boone,
What a mess to make in your mom's front room.
Joss sticks burning, a little pot smoking,
Drug addiction looming? Now you gotta be joking:
The age of innocence signed on the dole,
As an English market town discovered Rock & Roll.

CHAPTER SEVEN

Summertime Blues

It all boiled over, it was all too much, I cried tears of delight and laughed with despair. I was emotional, twitchy, a complete nervous fucking wreck. It was my last day of school at the County High. I had taken off my coat, my cap and my school tie and placed them in a tidy little pile on the front lawn outside the new swimming pool, still under construction, at the front of the school. I added a boxful of 45rpm singles to the pile and dowsed the lot in lighter fuel. I tossed a lighted match on the heap and the whole thing began to burn quite nicely. A crowd slowly gathered, then some of my mates turned up and added their uniforms to the inferno. All it needed was an effigy of E.J.S. Kyte, or even the real thing, and the symbolism was complete. I'd brought my records to school and had sold quite a few, given more away to deserving cases and the girl's I fancied, and set fire to the rest. A day that had started with a display of my commercial acumen, had progressed through philanthropy and bribery and now reached its climax in arson. To say my mood was volatile was a crushing understatement. So it was goodbye to the almost private school and hello to the totally public bar. I thought of Tom Browne leaving his school in a coach with horses, whilst I was leaving mine and going to the Coach and Horses. As the flames licked up into the clear sky, and the school motto burned on my blazer badge, a pint or two of Davenports seemed a bloody good idea. As a metaphor for life, appeared pretty spooky; Mom had always said 'When things get choppy for you, you always run to the drink'.

And it had all started so well.

My first three years had been spent in the original school building, with it's vast assembly hall, cantilevered classrooms, science laboratories housed in gothic mini-chapels, a full floor to ceiling library, complete with mobile ladders, and lecture rooms that would not have looked out of place in the British Museum. When I joined, the school still had separate play areas for the girls and boys, and these were kept apart by the 'temporary' single-storey classroom blocks. These were affectionately and accurately known as the A and B huts. The whole school was contained in a large grassed area, which supported two football pitches, hockey and netball facilities, and athletics track. All of this space was known as 'The Green', and games pitches were moved around each season, to take full advantage of the best unspoilt turf. Only one feature remained as a permanent structure, a diabolical instrument of pain and torture, the devil incarnate and terror of all first formers; the water jump. Whoever had designed the monster, was decidedly more at ease with the concept of the Grand National than the cross country run, and obviously had no greater feelings of generosity towards horses than children. I still vividly remember in my first-year run, lapping the school perimeter, blowing hard, legs on fire, my heart thumping against my chest, having completed what seemed like a tour of North Worcestershire's allotments and gated fields, to be confronted by this huge brushwood barrier standing guard over Lake Windermere. Having attempted to vault the fence, I succeeded only in ploughing through it, carrying thorny branches with me into the waiting reservoir. Half stumbling, half swimming, I completed the crossing and thanking the lord, fell over the finish line. Any boy that drowned, was considered to lack moral fibre and was deducted House points.

I enjoyed all the school games and athletics, and at various times captained my house football and cricket sides. Notwithstanding the water-jump, I relished cross country running and could usually get round the course on about five Embassy filter tipped, I was a competent miler and my high-jump, so I'm told, was a thing to behold. As I write this now, I think there must have been someone else in my body back then.

I have to say the rot had set in academically, so to speak, but not as yet across all fields of endeavour. I was relishing my English classes, discovering Hellespont swimmers and Warwickshire playwrights, Mr. Polly and D.H. Laurence, Winslow Boys and mellow, fruitfulness.

The sciences still held me in their thrall, not least because the lustrously wonderful Joyce Roberts used to sit on the end of her row, half way up the paddy-field stepped classroom, and, coming in to the lesson late, I always walked up the pyramid steps to the back of the class and could see right up her skirt as I made my lustful progress. Higher education indeed. I fantasized endlessly about her and found myself only attending the lessons that she did. I would have gladly given up my home and family to have joined her in the netball changing rooms. No wonder my curriculum was becoming less vitae. Eventually even Joyce couldn't keep me in the science classes, and my dismal exam marks eventually excluded me from all three; no more Bunsen burner fires, no more acid burns through the bench, the floor and quite possibly the ceiling below, and thankfully, no more bloody creature drawings.

The headmaster himself taught maths from year three onwards, whilst I played the jukebox in the Midland Café, until the Coach and Horses opened for business.

I took my 'O' levels in English Lit, English Lang and Geography and passed all three. On hearing my results, Kyte wittingly observed that a life on the road beckoned, as at least I could find my way around and be able to spell my destinations, in postcards back to my friends.

The Midland Café finally became my private study room, when, after one Saturday spent on the removal vans helping my dad, I returned to school on Monday to find, on the main notice board no less, that I had been excluded from all school sports teams, for failing to turn up that weekend for the under 16's. I had followed the normal procedure, when not available, and lodged my reasons well in advance of the game, to the sports master, at that time Percy Holbrook. He denied receiving it, Kyte accepted his word and even intervention by George Mills couldn't rescue me.

So now in my final year, with no games to pursue, and only six periods to attend in the whole week, my education really stalled. But my darts and cribbage improved. On two days of the week I had no lessons at all, so I attended the register role-call, then gave the 'Midland' my undivided attention. Nobody seemed to care.

'Only the Lonely', 'Peter Gunn' and 'Hit the road Jack', were the late summer's big hits. Matt Gibblin was the towns 'hard knock' and used to sit in the corner of the café, on his own, drinking cola, then eating the glass. What a prat, what a diet, what about when he went to the loo? He really was a pane in the arse. He was a real street fighting bastard, who'd jumped off the dodgems one night when the fair was in town, and decided to grace Bromsgrove with his debonair charm. He terrorised the local kids, until one night, walking home from school, we met him blocking the footpath. 'Stay out of the café, or I'll fucking 'ammer all of yer'. That was all he said that night on the school drive, before my best mate Roger 'Duke' Witherford, broke his nose, knocked out half his teeth and blacked both his eyes.

Roger was a stunningly good bloke. He knew more about rock n' roll records than anyone I've ever known. He used to listen to Luxemburg and AFN all night, every night, and every Friday he'd bring out his own top twenty chart and pin it on the detention board. Nobody ever dared to take it down. Not even the staff. He kept a book with every record release logged and detailed. When I met him at an Everly Brothers concert over forty years later, he'd still got it. He told me though that he'd finally given up his listings in 1980.

Roger wore the most fabulous Teddy Boy gear; black Italian suits with really tight drain-pipe trousers, three quarter coats with red velvet half-moon pockets, marvellous coloured shirts (when white was the only colour you could buy), 'slim jim' tie, 'bumper' shoes and fluorescent socks. He wore black rimmed Buddy Holly glasses and sported the biggest hair-do with a quiff and 'ducks-arse'. Looking like that you had to be a fighting man, and although a good-natured and gentle friend to be with, in a rough house he was powerful and extremely dangerous. He ruled Rubery and south Birmingham from the age of fifteen with a pretty violent bunch of psychopaths. I don't know where it all came from. He wasn't really tall or stockily built, and his eyesight was chronic. Christ only knows what he would have done to Gibblin if he could have seen him.

This then was the era of rock, the 'Duke', underage drinking, and bollocks to school.

So after one brief year climbing the ladder, I spent the next four, sliding ever faster down the snakes.

I wasn't really a duffer, but I think you have to have a sort of love affair with your school, and mine was just an infatuation, a brief encounter that didn't grow to become anything of any real substance.

When any love turns sour, it much quicker becomes willful and dismissive. I took against the teaching staff and imagined some personal vendetta against me, my upbringing, my even being at the school. Perhaps it wasn't all imagination, but it all ran out of my control.

I was by turn Jack the lad and Jack the sad. It wasn't helpful that my reputation mirrored the great dancer Mr. Bojangles, but only inasmuch as 'he drinks a bit'. Classroom clown, public bar fly, part time Edwardian street fighter, closet poet, general fucking mess. I was about to save myself from oblivion by riding round the country in rickety rackety furniture vans, drinking with vagrants, finding a good girl, settling down, paying a mortgage, taking up knitting, learning Swahili, having a sex-change. That was the plan.

No, that was never the plan.

As I walked away from the pyre of my vanities, and left the school for the last time, a classmate shook my hand and said 'Good luck Neath, thanks for the record'. I'd given him Eddie Cochran's 'Summertime Blues'.

Many years after that day on the lawn, when my eyesight was still poor, but I could see so much better, I bought the record again at a music fair in Cheltenham. I still think it's great, and it's not sad anymore. Memory's rose-coloured spectacles can pick out the gold in the cold of my schooldays, but no, they were not the best days of my life.

CHAPTER EIGHT

Whole lotta shakin' at the Queens

When I first heard Jerry Lee Lewis "Great balls of fire", it left my senses reeling, like I'd been beaten up with an adrenalin hammer. That pumping piano intro, 'you shake my nerves and you rattle my brain', he shook and rattled mine to pieces, still does, every time I hear it.

The NME carried the news, Jerry was coming to England. I'd commit mass murder at the box office to get a ticket. Then three dates into the tour, before he got to Birmingham, he was going back home in disgrace.

It was all because of Myra.

In the southern states of America, it's not unusual to see pictures in the wedding album of the groom, the bride and his sister, and only count two people. They have close-knit family groups down Tennessee way and in difficult swampy terrain, when a man's looking for a wife, it cuts down on difficult travelling, if there's a relative who can do the job.

I'm sorry, that's bigoted statement and I shouldn't say such things, but it makes me laugh; anyway it wasn't quite so shocking with Jerry, he just married his cousin; God knows it's a national sport with our own aristocracy, but what really tugged the hypocrisy bell with the British press was her age. She was only fourteen; but very pretty. Today she'd either be a super model, or a game-show hostess; cover of 'Hello', the face of Farleys Rusks, the world would be her plaything.

"Fame is the spur that the clear spirit doth raise.........
And slits the thin spun life".

Theatres cancelled his engagements, TV and radio shunned him, he was hounded out of the Country. It was to be three years until he returned, like most American acts, including the giants of Rock n' Roll, Jerry's record sales had gone into free-fall thanks to the Beatles and Mersey beat. But at least Myra was seventeen now, so everything in the garden was rosy, persecution-wise.

Martin Cox, Albert Adams "Shocker Jock", he was of the Scottish persuasion, and myself, had got hold of three of the hottest tickets in town, and were up in Brum to make an early start in the pre-prandial wall-pissing championships.

First call was the Discery in Hurst Street, the definitive record shop in town, where, after a few pleasantries with the boss, you could grab an armful of LP's and repair to a listening booth upstairs, for the duration, if you had that sort of time on your hands. It was appreciated if you actually bought something and as I was now a regular and learning all about jazz, alphabetically, and had only reached John Coltrane and Ornette Coleman and other C-listers, I dared not abuse his hospitality, with twenty three letters still to come.

Anyway, I'd always have USA Rock n' Roll records on order, and most of them were imported for us, with only a minimal charge. We kept this little arrangement a secret, and our street 'cred' in the record-buying world amongst the other kids, was sky high.

Martin was still busy amassing Bromsgrove's definitive drum-solo, long playing record collection, and was continuing this mission with an ever deepening interest in black magic. This was the dark satanic arts, not the chocolates. I guess that at this time if he could have found a hitherto un-catalogued recording of the Beelzebub Quartet featuring Buddy Rich, his life would have been one long infernal, demonic jam session. Up styx and away, so to speak. Our listening done, orders placed and purchases bagged, we left the shop for 'The House of Liang Nam'. This wasn't the sequel to the Animals chart success about a New Orleans residence, but a fabulous Chinese restaurant in the shadow of New Street Station.

After spending about six months sampling what was then a new cultural experience, and due to shyness, ignorance and stupidity, only ever ordering chicken fried rice, this place was the opening door to the real Chinese culinary experience. The staff were friendly, helpful and only too pleased to try out all their exotic combinations, on the three imbeciles from the country. They obviously possessed a compelling necessity to bring a wider appreciation of oriental dining pleasures to teenage West Midland hotheads.

So, having established the ground rules, being that they would serve us with a dozen or so different dishes, and we would sample them, discuss their merits, rate them on the overall pleasure scale, and of course pay for them, the Cantonese cornucopia began to fill the table.

We sat in wide-eyed amazement round the lazy susan (or would that be razy suzie?), as the banquet was distributed around the server in it's individual bowls. This was truly our road to Damascus, or maybe the road to Hong Kong, anyway, one of the Hope and Crosby films, and a million miles from 'one from column A, one from column B'.

With our side plates of fried and boiled rice, we sat around the table, playing Chinese roulette, eagerly trying all the dishes, until we were totally gorged. Martin entertained us and the staff, with a drum solo on the chopsticks, which only masked the fact that he didn't know how to eat with them.

I think the irony was lost on Martin, when Albert suggested that his solo's when playing in the band, sounded like he was wielding cutlery.

Now with the clock showing two roman numerals, it was indeed time to cross the city and insinuate ourselves into a wondrously diverse pub the Chapel, in I think, Newhall Street. This was a pub with a very big, built-in secret.

A proper Brum pub; shoulder to shoulder busy, full of side-splitting jokery told in plangent, flat accents, glass clinking, beer-spilling, belly laughing, smoke-billowing uproar.

Yet somewhere through the laughter, the chatter and the blue smoke haze, came the delicate, magical, floating notes of a Mozart violin concerto. It was as unexpected as an educated footballer arriving in a late train on the wrong platform in Zurich railway station. Shouting in a controlled whisper across the bar, we managed to order three pints of M and B each, and also discovered that the entire City of Birmingham Symphony Orchestra were upstairs in the assembly room, practising for the next evening's concert.

We climbed the stairs at the back of the bar, and opening a double door at the top, found ourselves in a huge, wooden-floored room. With few windows and the paintwork dulled by the smoke from Victorian mill-workers' cigars, and more contemporary shop-steward's woodbines, it was almost like walking onto the deck of a nineteenth century warship. Arranged in crescent formation on the poop deck, were the CBSO, enjoying a break-time pint. We were outnumbered by real musicians by about ten to one.

A waiter brought our drinks up and we sat back and listened, as the orchestra put on a free gala performance just for us.

The beer, the Chinese banquet, Mozart and the slowly lengthening shadows, as the hall turned pink, then red, created a surreal reverie in that old room above the distant clamour of the real, rowdy world below.

With the music still echoing in our heads, we stumbled out into the early evening streets and weaved our way across the Cathedral lawn towards Victoria Square. This night we were to be entertained by three piano maestro's of the twentieth century, at the Town Hall.

In an orderly melee, we flowed like a good-natured, jostling amoeba, along the Town Hall's portico's; bumping without the balance of sobriety, literally from pillar to post. I always had the feeling, in this building, that I was in above-ground catacombs; propelled by the friendly, but insistent mob, up flights of stairs, around corners, finally to emerge like toothpaste out of a tube, onto the balcony overlooking the curtain-hidden stage. Almost before we had settled in our seats, the house lights dimmed, the crowd's expectant hubbub was slipping into controlled hysteria. Imperceptibly, through the half-light, the curtain began to rise. No spot-lights. Then a heavy, base note piano chord, a thick, blues voice, "I'm walking to New Orleans........" At last a blue-white beam picked out the big man at his seat; Hysteria changed gear, pandemonium roared round the balcony. The whole auditorium screamed out the name, Fats Domino. The backbeat was insistent, compelling. "I've got my knapsack on my back", Fats was on a roll, so was the balcony. All our feet, thudding down in unison, the place began to tremble. I thought "it won't just be your knapsack on your back, Antoine, if this keeps going on."

All the while, the curtain kept slowly rising, Fats blasted on, we were going to demolish the first floor balcony for sure. Impossible; through the gloom, another piano began to appear, on top of the first one. A white face, a moustache, a huge bouffant, screaming out of the second spotlight, "You keep a knockin, but you can't come in......" Sweet Jesus, Little Richard. The tremble turned into a full-on bounce. The girls were trying to outscream Richard, Fats was still walkin', people were thumping each other in uncontrollable passion; I looked at my two mates, we couldn't speak, it was synchronised mayhem.

The curtain was still rising. It couldn't be true, a third piano began to form on top of the other two, a lions mane of blonde hair caught in spotlight number three, "Come alonga honey, whole lotta shakin' goin' on......" Fucking Mary Magdalen, it was the 'killer' Jerry Lee himself, smashing into the chords, standing up, his right foot on the keyboard. Richard was still knockin', Fats still walkin', everybody earning eternal glory with apostrophes. The whole wonderful Hall was alive. Everyone was punching the air, jumping, hugging, crying, swearing, laughing, stamping out the beat. The place was going to crumble around us, we were all going to die, be buried alive with our rock n' roll heroes. The tombstone would be three white concert grand pianos, one atop the other, the epitaph: "Gone but never forgotten, 'Walkin', Shakin', knockin' for ever."

We all survived to tell the tale of the greatest rock concert ever heard. Neither the old concert hall nor all the people privileged to be there on that night, have ever seen a night like it, before or since.

The old lady has just come back to life, after a lengthy refurbishment and looks as fresh and pristine as she must have done when Mendelssohn visited. I hope there are many more magical nights here, on into the next century. I certainly remember many concerts here, this one above all, with a mystical warmth, the hall and its audience becoming a living entity.

Apart from the bruises, the loss of my voice, the two day headache, three day tinnitus, and the birth of a life-long fear of being inside neo-classical buildings, a perfect night. And Jerry Lee never tried to shoot anybody.

And so to the après-ski, so to speak. Although bewildered by our sonic battering, there was still time to grab a couple of drinks before the last train to next day.

In the sixties, the railway companies' grand hotel's were still a reality, albeit a quickly fading one, and New Street Station still boasted two, the Midland and the Queens, which stared at each other across Corporation Street. This old Queen had certainly seen better days, her fittings, like the building itself, were tired and frowsy, but she still wore her tiara, now tarnished and at a rather too-jaunty angle. The hotel was an integral part of the station itself, before the whole site was demolished, to be rebuilt as an underground public convenience, with all the ambiance of a refugee camp.

How ironic that the railway and its hotel's were all created to offer succour, comfort and even luxury to its' passengers, where now there is only stark and hideous coldness and a constant stream of metallic humanoid threats and warnings, with overt promises of penalties and internment for any petty misdemeanour, that its cowed and bullied 'customers' may commit. The day-long, continuous haranguing, interspersed with insincere and meaningless messages of apology for the late or non appearance of the inhumanly overcrowded and grossly inadequate trains, make my blood chill and I think of Aldous Huxley "O brave new world, with people like this in it."

It was here, in the Gentlemen's Bar of the Queens, that the three amigos pitched up for their last couple of nightcaps.

As Martin and I sat back and relived the wonders of the earlier evening, 'Shocker' went up for three pints of Worthington. He came back with a Tom Collins, a Sidecar and a Blue Nile. "For fuck sake 'Shocker', we wanted a pint each, not an Irish rebel, a motorbike accessory and an African River." A row ensued. Ok, we agreed it was Michael Collins, not Tom, and that the Blue and the White Nile both were counted as the one, for the purpose of measuring its length, but bloody hellfire, these were women's drinks, cocktails, what were you thinking man.

We drank them, after all 'Shock' had paid for them, and grudgingly we agreed they tasted alright.

Martin went up to bring us back the real stuff, and we all tried a Screwdriver for size.

My round consisted of two Pimms, and I succumbed to another Blue Nile. I think I ought to make clear at this point, that none of us had lost the power of speech totally, nor the wit to order the drinks that we desired, but the Bar Mistress, for this she truly was, was of an earlier and more elegant age, and longed to return to same. She was also of a most persuasive nature, charming, flattering, alluring and absolutely irresistible to such young, rough trade as we. If you went to her bar and demanded a pint of lager, then a Pimms No.2 is what you got.

So everybody was happy.

From this confusing and not originally encouraging beginning, the Gentlemen's bar, together with the queen of the Queens, became great favourites of ours.

We were regulars, making a beeline for the place as soon as kicking-out time occurred at the Odeon or the Town Hall.

Strangely we never asked her name and she never proffered it. It has to be admitted, someone who knew that much about drinks, and, a woman........., we were totally in awe of her.

So now we knew our 'Bloody Mary' from our 'Cuba Libre', and that not all drinks came in pint pots. We learned a little bit about fascinating women and had perhaps turned the first page of the book of finer things in life. We were almost rubbing shoulders, albeit ever so gingerly, with elegance, wit and decorum.

It looked like a long, long road leading away from Highfield Road, but I was beginning to prefer it to the A38.

Our lady also knew the signalman well on platform thirteen, and he used to give her a quick phone-call, when our train was five minutes from the off.

Jerry Lee had given us the shaking, our lady at the Queens had begun to stir us.

Birmingham Town Hall. Photograph courtesy of Leonard
Stace, www.photobydjnorton.com

CHAPTER NINE

Dead Poet Society

Ernie Hodgkiss was a small bloke. My friend Martin said, "He starts at fuck-all and tapers off". It was a bit unfair. A bit, but not much. He was a big ego in a little body and fitted comfortably into the old comedy monologue, "most of the world's greatest men were small; Hitler, Napoleon, Stalin, Crippen etc. etc." I don't think Ernie wanted to rule the world, but he thought Emperor of Bromsgrove might make a fitting title.

It was in Perry Hall, one time home of A.E. Housman, that Martin and I first became aware of this mercurial midget. The old place had scrubbed up well and its faded elegance created the perfect backdrop for the town's upwardly mobile set. Several couples were engaged in sotto voce conversation, whilst we made our way to a corner table, and began to plan the forthcoming attack on the High Street pubs.

Into this haven of sophisticated understatement, strutted the tiny tornado. "Power dressing" hadn't been invented in the 60's, but he was doing it anyway. An eye-catching black cord suit with three-quarter frock-coat and drainpipe trousers, black dinner shirt and white tie, and black socks in chukka boots announced his arrival. The whole ensemble was topped with a sable Cossack hat, worn at a jaunty angle. The lion in winter; except that this was a balmy early evening in late summer.

As he crossed the lounge with barely an acknowledgement to the barman, he shouted out his drink order, greeted several of the seated couples in profane manner and throwing his hat to the floor, sat down at the table in the centre of the room. I thought he was the corgi's scrotum. It deserved a round of applause. It was also interesting when the waiter brought his drink over, especially as there was no waiter-service at Perry Hall. Until now.

I'd wondered why Housman had written 'A Shropshire Lad' when he was a Worcestershire boy, but now his "blue remembered hills" served only as a rhyming couplet with Ernie's black September frills. Martin had met him a couple of times before and soon we were insinuated into his company. This company began to arrive as the evening wore on and the foundation was laid for mob-handed toping on a grand scale. To say I never drew sober breath between Friday and Sunday for over two years, may be something of an exaggeration, but if so, it's only because the accompanying amnesia made exact record keeping a hit and miss affair.

This marked the beginning of the 'High Street Raffle Run', where everyone would write on a ticket the number of pubs we would visit that night, and how many of us would finish the course. The cards were all left behind the bar at Perry Hall and checked out the next evening. It was always exciting, as no-one could ever remember what they had predicted, and as we didn't put our names on the cards, nobody knew who, if anyone, had won. What a piss-poor way to run a raffle; however, predating the Camelot version by some years, I feel that our prototype, where we had a good drink before we knew the outcome, and then in fact, never knew that outcome, was far more satisfactory than the later model, where depression and disappointment on a weekly basis actually has to be paid for.

Our nights out often began at Ernie's house, watching Dr. Who. William Hartnell in a smoking jacket and a night-cap, Papier mache dustbins, exterminating the universe with plungers that unblocked the sink, floating around like slow motion dervishes, but with no ability to travel in an upward direction.

The thought had occurred to some of us, that to avoid vaporisation, all you had to do was go upstairs. Just imagine, the final episode, the Earth's population has been wiped out, except for five hundred Brummies, holding out valiantly in a first floor flat in Chelmsley Wood. Of course they'd finally be overwhelmed when somebody went down for a packet of fags and the Sunday paper, and left the lift door open. On the occasions when we got to 'the Hall' before Ernie, when he was late, fishing in somebody's garden pond, as Martin unkindly used to say, he'd always enter with his customary greeting, "Flash you, clear three tables". Nobody ever did, but one night a persecuted waiter said to him, "If it's as big as your mouth, nobody's got a fucking chance". Harsh words, but dashed close to the truth.

All in all he was a bastard; but he was our bastard, and knew all the pub gaffers, the 'stoppy-backs' and the sweetest barmaids, and because of him, I came to meet some of the most interesting people in the town, many of whom became my good, life-lasting friends.

Roger Annetts was immortalised as 'mini-man', not because he was an Ernie clone, but for his ownership of Alec Issigonis's miracle of modern science, the Austin mini. At a time when all the young people in the town who owned a car would fit inside a telephone box, every Friday night we'd get all the people who would fit inside a telephone box into Roger's car. Then, in our transport of delight, the six or seven of us would thrash down the M5 to Strensham services for a sausage sandwich and a coffee, and slam our way back up to town for the serious business of the night, like sleeping, or lying in the bushes at Housman's ex abode.

It was quite cramped, and a useful trick was the ability to breath through glass. To an observer, if ever there was one, when we passed, the car must have looked like a jar of pickled onions. Driving under these conditions, was a singular skill; some nights Roger got a foot on one of the pedals, some nights not. One evening he never touched the steering wheel with either hand, until we were coming up the slip-road at about seventy miles an hour.

The car was also an aid to romance and Roger became extremely popular with the local beauties, who hitherto had been forced to walk to the local coffee bar for their drink and sausage sandwich. His street-cred went off the Richter scale when he not only 'pulled' a much lusted over lady from the Golden Lion, called Primrose, but rumour had it, he also managed her sister Rosemary. It became common knowledge in the town, that Roger was mad about fucking flowers. Roger was a real gentleman, always convivial and engaging. It was easy to see how he managed to keep his plant garden well cultivated. It was also inevitable that decency would overpower and eventually claim him, as he spiralled downwards into respectability and finally marriage. The M5 grand prix's and mini escapades slipped into misty memory.

Our trawl through the taverns thus returned to pedestrian mode, with many an unsuspecting landlord subjected to an impromptu evening of colourful folk singing. These nights would often climax with a full choral rendition of the 'Queen Street Girls', and on special occasions, an Ernie solo on 'She stood on the bridge at midnight'. As other chapters give testimony, music has always been a golden thread running through the fabric of my life. So along with our volga-hatted vocalist, like pictures in an exhibition, came other heroes.

Roy Duffell was insane, but he was a bloody good milkman. Roy was always late to join the gang and quite often early to leave, but only because he never knew what time it was. A fatal flaw, one would suppose, in the career ambitions of a milkman, but townspeople on Roy's round, all gave glowing testimony to his punctuality and efficiency. Perhaps he had an identical twin, who kept him locked in the cellar between 5am and 8pm.

He'd arrive in the lounge, always flushed, always twitchy, an uncontrollable bundle of nervous energy. Bundle is a pretty apt description of a man who always seemed to be wearing other people's cloths, that he'd come upon at a jumble sale for the colour-blind. When I say other peoples, I don't mean, say, a fireman's helmet, ski-boots and a bra, but it was a close run thing. Pullovers, he seemed to hold in special affection. Enormous pullovers, whose multi-coloured patterns needed sun-glass attention, knitted by giant needles, that allowed letters to be posted through the stitches, and sagged down below his knees, like woollen swimming trunks, after a walk in the sea. Jeans whose turn-ups had parted company with his footwear by the odd six inches, revealing socks never of a matching pair, and shoes, or something like them, sometimes of the same size, occasionally of the same colour, and seldom of the same sort. He was certainly a conversation stopper, as he marched into the piano bar each Friday. When he did at last join us and calm down long enough to take a drink, he'd begin his brilliant, apocryphal monologues about his customers on the round. People listening in were sucked into his spider's web of conversation, enthralled as he spun tale after tale of dairyland fantasy. Like the dumb Welshman ordering his milk and eggs by means of the deaf people's hand code. Roy said he came from a welsh miming village.

The stories kept coming, Roy was into his stride and virtually unstoppable. His audience marvelled at the panoply of characters paraded through the lounge and must have thought Roy's milk round was a circuit tour of the comedy store. It was of course nothing of the sort, but a pretty run down part of the town, whose only ray of sunshine was its milkman. None of it was true, but he inhabited this wonderland and brought it vividly to life, to all the hypnotised audiences, night after night.

Almost by accident, I discovered something else about our dreadfully dressed roundsman; he was an encyclopaedia of Modern Jazz knowledge and had what must have been one of the great record collections of the age.

It came about one early evening, I walked into an almost deserted bar and noticed Roy, alone in the window-seat. He was muttering away to himself twenty to the dozen and looked, and sounded, clearly troubled. "What's the problem mate?" "You'll never believe this Bruce, I was out on the round this morning......" his voice trailed off into silence. I wondered what tragedy had befallen him, had he knocked someone down with the milk-cart, had there been an unpleasant scene, perhaps a road accident, I couldn't guess. "I was out at about five thirty, I was humming a tune, happy to be alive, you know...." "Whatever happened Roy?" "Bruce, I was humming a fucking TV advert."

I couldn't grasp the import of this admittance, but then it all came tumbling out, how he knew the complete song-books of Berlin, Porter, Rodgers and Hart, Carmichael and Gershwin; had catalogued the entire recorded output of Ella, Sarah Vaughan, Peggy Lee, Billy Holliday, could sing very passable impressions of Sinatra, Martin, Nat Cole and Tony Bennett, and after pressing my enquiries deeper, I discovered he'd been trilling, "I'm the Veno's snowman, call me Pop, you'll find me in the chemist shop."

He could barely contain his rage and his shame. I suppose it was like Mozart waking up one morning with the 'Crossroads' theme running through his head. Much later that night, after seven or eight pints of Bass had dulled the pain of embarrassment, we went back to his flat, where I was overwhelmed to find his whole apartment was one very full, floor to ceiling, record shop. There were literally thousands of singles, EP's, LP's, the whole spectrum of Jazz, since the early forties and right up to date. American and South African, French and Belgian imports, including very rare limited editions.

He gave me Leonard Feather's introduction to the music and musicians, and set me on the life-time love affair with the whole genre. He was a warm and generous man, just mad enough to be a truly special person. I'm forever in his debt, and god help him, I still find myself whistling the 'Veno's snowman' jingle even today.

Lochlan Gilmore and I had finished our sausage sandwiches in the Bristol Road Transport Café in Longbridge and returned to his scrapyard escapee, or Austin 1100 as the log book described it. "It's time I changed this, I've had my eye on a Ford V8 Pilot." Putting Loch, cars and driving into the same sentence, was sure to preface some pretty frightening saga of carnage and mayhem, and that was usually before he'd changed into second gear. Adding a V8 motor to the mix made me blanche at the thought of what terror could be in store.

We sat with the motor running, then Loch, peering through the rear-view mirror, said "Here comes my new car Bruce." He pulled out, tyres screaming, into the road, fifty yards in front of an approaching Jaguar. Fifty yards further on, he slammed on what remained of the Austin's brakes and shouted "Hold fucking tight." With the smell of burning rubber in our nostrils, the jalopy came to a halt. So did the Jag, but not fast enough. He hit us fair and square and our car fell apart, like a circus-car clown act. In a blinding storm of cigarette ash, the windscreen sprang out, the car chassis broke in half just behind the two front seats, and the passenger's door fell off.

Now sitting at 45 degrees, clutching the remains of the dashboard, I gazed at the open sky and as the last hub-cap rolled away down the highway, a water-hissing silence descended on the scene. This little cameo was the prelude to Lochlan's insurance claim, citing a jay-walker whose life he heroically saved, whilst throwing both his and mine, into jeopardy at the same time. He expressed some sad surprise that the pedestrian had failed to stay at the scene long enough to thank him, and naturally sympathised with the Jaguar driver. However he had failed to stop and hit us from behind. He of course never mentioned that he'd taken the rear stop lights out of the Austin. As I extricated myself from what was now an Austin 550, I considered myself fortunate to have joined a growing band of Lochlan's insurance claim survivors.

These were easily identifiable in the bars of Bromsgrove. They were to be seen shambling in during the early evening, unsteady on their feet, prone to stumble, shaky of hand, shifty-eyed and exhibiting a nervous tic, with a tendency to periodically spin round and survey the scene behind them. Those who still possessed hair grew it long, lank and predominately grey. Not difficult to miss, for blokes in their early twenties.

Loch had perfected this modus operandi and had successfully executed the ploy on several occasions. The chances of becoming a 'V8 Pilot' owner looked ever rosier. He used a lot of insurance companies, who knew he was a bad risk, but thought him extremely unlucky. He also knew a lot of ex-passengers who thought he was a suicidal bastard. But there was much more to Loch than automobile felony. His public-school education had stimulated his already enquiring mind, and combined with a burning energy, marked him down as a future man of stature, or more likely, an international criminal. Of course, if politics had taken his fancy, it could conceivably combine the two.

It's all about qualifications; I'm reminded of two stories, the first, when the writer Graham Greene was interviewed by the editor of the Evening Standard regarding the post of political correspondent. He asked Greene why he wanted the job, to be told that he was interested in Politics and was sure his burgeoning writing style would be appreciated by his readers. "Right," said the editor, "Then who is the foreign secretary?" "Christ, I said I was interested, not obsessed" said Greene. He failed to land the job. The other concerned Rex Harrison, the actor, who apparently belied his screen persona as a cuddly, lovable, charming sort of fellow. At a swish party one evening, he was buttonholed by a political journalist, who asked him which party he voted for. "None of them," replied Harrison, "they're all cunts." "Well, most of the British people of cunts," replied the journo, "and they do deserve representation, you know."

Loch would disappear from the scene for months on end, to reappear with the announcement of a 'coming home' party. These were legendary, not to mention interesting. 'Substances' became available along with imported, perfumed girls, who it seemed, were always keen to play your favourite tracks from the Stones' latest album. With Lock holding court like a holy man, his flat became a little part of Bromsgrove that was forever India; at least for a few weeks, then the show would move onto the road again. The town was never going to be big enough for him, there were larger rooms to brighten, more expensive cars to terminate. I wish him well, wherever he is; probably an English speaking gang-master in a Philippino porno-Barbie Doll manufacturing sweatshop, living in a luxury hill station bungalow, reading Proust, and driving a vintage Daimler-Jaguar, very carefully.

Colin Giles was the 'cool-maester' of the town during the awfully named 'Swinging Sixties'. It sounds like everyone spent the decade in a children's playground. What a different connotation that thought was today, when apparently everyone's next door neighbour is a paedophile.

It's not just nostalgia that draws me back, like all of us, to those childhood days, when the worst thing a kid could contemplate was a visit, every fortnight, by the 'nit-nurse'. Sic transit Gloria mondi. "Love me do" was number twelve in the charts, but Colin had a green velvet jacket with no lapels, long before the Beatles. They must have known his tailor, an Italian in Kings Heath, Birmingham.

Ernie had sensationally caused uproar in Perry Hall lounge, when after being asked to leave, apparently because of lewd behaviour, he had suggested to Tony Cabot, the new manager, that he had more right to be there than he, as he'd been selling melons on the runway at Menorca airport only a few short weeks ago.

Eloquently claiming that Ernie was in no way either anti-spanish, or indeed fruitist, but merely tired, emotional and a bloody nuisance, Colin put forward a compelling case for clemency, but when this was brutally rejected, we all did the noble supportive thing and told him to stick his paella up his arse, along with the 'Red Barrel' and the society moved on, to the Golden Lion.

We had of course been erstwhile visitors, but things had changed. The two pub 'flowers', Rosemary and Primrose, had moved to another bed, Roger's, and the place had split into two distinct factions. The back bar was the fevered world of Rock n' Roll, Johnny Kidd and the Pirates, U.S. Bonds and the Drifters, pouring high volume out of the Wurlitzer juke-box, the little room full of motorbike riders, motorbike leathers, and occasionally the motorbikes as well. In the front lounge, the new Trad Jazz boom had gripped the white wine set, and the place was haunted by freaks in hacking jackets with leather elbow patches, horn-rimmed specs, pipes and beards, and that was just the women.

We tossed a coin and settled for the front lounge. Even women with beards were better than blokes who only washed every month, whether they needed it or not, and who wore Castrol oil for aftershave. It only remained to get Roy so drunk, that he lost the will to wage 'Jazz War' against these new infidels, and we began to fit as comfortably into our new environment, as a steak-pie into a fat bloke's mouth.

Colin and I became great friends and besides the pleasures of single malt whiskies and morrocan marijuana, he also introduced me to Gambling Jack, Quig the Queer and Slick Slaney and the Germans. These were not exotically named west midlands rock bands, but new members of the continually expanding society.

Gambling Jack was always in the lounge. Never at all fazed by the Jazz crowd, he still retained a small niche in the bar corner, ever willing to impart his turf information for the price of a pint. He was a sort of stool-sat, tic-tac tosspot. The pub was next door to the bookies, and Jack had the air of a man at ease with life and himself. He had come to terms with the two passions of his existence, beer and horses, and had found Valhalla in the Golden Lion. I think he lived in the cellar.

At each evening's end we sat like disciples at the feet of the messiah, furiously scribbling those names that meant the passport to riches. Next morning the frantic, desperate attempts to decipher the pissed-up hieroglyphics of the night before. Sometimes we won, mostly we lost. The sport of kings remains so, whilst the poor keep giving them most of their money.

It was one such evening, whilst sitting on the floor opposite Jack, that I suddenly realised I could see the bottoms of his feet, and he'd still got his shoes on. I thought, Christ, if he's the best tipster in town, how long before I'm sitting here with him, stark fucking naked. It was my moment on the racing road to Damascus, I caught the bus back home. Jack kept on walking down the road, barefoot. 'Quig the Queer' was a peripheral member of the gang, mainly because, although he had a wonderfully attractive and joyously social wife, he was such a mind-blowing perfectionist, nobody could stand to be in his company for more than thirty seconds. His nickname had nothing to do with his sexual preference, but from the fact that he took fastidiousness from an art form to a science. He was the only man I've ever known that ironed creases in his Wellington boots.

I still have a mental picture of Quig and his wife Christine, whose blonde bouffant hair style made Dusty Springfield look bald, standing together in the changing coloured lights of the bonfire, at a Guy Fawkes party. Both of them were dressed in white suits (in November!) and green welly boots. They sported perfectly coiffed hair creations and Quig continually flapped away any invading spark, or insect, with a stylish matching white silk handkerchief. As the firelight played on their perfect profiles, they looked like gothic saints, and would not have looked out of place in alcoves on either side of the west window of Worcester cathedral. Or as the parents, in the sequel of "Village of the Damned."

Slick Slaney was an old 'Scout and School' friend of my cousin John and both had joined the Royal Navy, almost on the same day, when both were still in their teens.

Slick made almost meteoric progress in 'the mob' and every time he came home on leave, he seemed to have a higher rank and own another capital ship. This was in stark contrast to John, who always came home a stoker, and often was lucky to come home at all. This may have been because Slick viewed the Naval ranking system as a challenge, to be taken on and overcome, whilst John saw it as a toffee-nosed load of bastards. Exit left, fifteen years later, Commander Slaney; exit right, Killick Stoker Neath.

Slick was a pleasant, good natured, straight-up sort of guy. The sort of credentials that doomed him, as a long-serving society member. It didn't help that his mom was courting a serving German officer (she was widowed, but that was no excuse). Erwin was a decent sort of guy, but everybody called him 'Rommel'. I know its awfully politically incorrect, but this was only twenty years after the end of the war, and most of us, including me, reckoned World War II was politically incorrect. Nobody then was worrying about addresses and job titles, when most of the planet was still smouldering or destroyed, after the last annual general meeting got out of hand.

Our naval member was decent and honest, good fun, but already beginning to step back and think his way forward. Of course, he was a serving naval officer. He had one or two tricks still up his sleeve to show us, but his days as a fully paid-up society member were already numbered. No longer an itinerant piss-artist, but the sort of chap we wanted to be in command of our fighting ships. Could be Admiral Slaney (Ret.) by now.

I introduced Colin into this narrative; I've skipped round him, passed him by and intermittently come back to him. Because he's always there.

Because he always was. He was a constant, a source of joy, a revelation of knowledge, a tutor of serenity. I grew up in his presence, I was at ease with him, I trusted him implicitly. He became the first finger of my hand that I could always count on; that I could always rely on, in any dire circumstances.

As life thunders on, sometimes I'm driving it, sometimes it's dragging me along in its eternal path. I have still a few fingers on my hand that I know I can count on. There's never been more than five. Colin's is still the first one.

So whilst perhaps not Chaucer, the "Milkman's Tale", and "Mad Fucker on the Bristol Road's Tale", have a certain 1960's frisson.

There was an exciting momentum to those days, a thrilling expectation, as we were all about to burst away from the cosy confines of each others' company, like a fuse-burning Catherine wheel. I can feel it even now.

More the rights of a piss age than a rite of passage.

CHAPTER TEN

Skin Deep

It was said in Bromsgrove's tonsorial society, that the pudding basin was invented to match Billy O'Brien's hair cuts. The recipients of his barber-shop skills, or 'victims' as they were more widely known, were instantly recognisable all over the town.

To stroll up the High Street on Friday 'half price day', was akin to taking a pre-vespers promenade through a monastery's cloisters, where all the fraternity were in mufti. Billy was also likely to snip off a piece of ear-lobe, scar the nape of the neck and dig the scissors into the scalp; that was providing he hadn't been in heavy conversation with a bottle of Jameson's whiskey the night before. Had that indeed been the case, he would send his clients out into the streets looking like war heroes. On any weekday afternoon, if a man was espied stumbling along the highway, blood streaming from what looked like a vicious head-wound and a glazed, fearful expressions in his eyes, he'd either been drinking and had fallen into the path of an oncoming car, or he'd had his hair cut at Billy's.

All of us kids went to Billy's and all grew up with the unusually short ears to prove it. The O'Brien's had one son, Mick, and two dogs. On hair cut day, Mick used to make grand entrances into the chair-room, with swords, rifles, tactical nuclear missiles, and any other weapons of warfare that he could lay his hands on. Where they all came from I have never found out. We'd all be sitting on the hard leather benches around the perimeter of the room, whilst Billy worked his sanguine way round the chair, up to his knees in hair and Bonio biscuits. Mick would describe a circle round the room, lunging, slashing and swirling away with a claymore or a broadsword, or whatever was available on that particular day.

Two men, one old and drunk, the other young and mad, out of control, with extremely sharp pieces of steel, in a room not much bigger than a telephone box. Hellfire, when I saw 'Psycho' a few years later, I thought the shower scene was a pretty dull cameo. Truman Capote could have followed up 'In Cold Blood', if he'd ever researched the Bromsgrove

Hairdressers' Directory, and obtained eye-witness statements of a normal day in the cutting room, so to speak. He could have called it 'In Long Hair', or something like.

This rambling preamble serves as introduction to Mick O'Brien, who, although completely manic when attached to something sharp and shiny, was also a naturally gifted musician. It came to pass that one day, one of Billy's customers left, in payment for his disfigurement, an alto saxophone. Mick picked it up and when he discovered it had no cutting edge, began to play it.

At about this time, Martin and I had begun to discover modern jazz, well, I'd begun to discover it and Martin had become obsessed with drummers. No any old drummers, but the great 'showman' drummers of the swing era; Max Roach, Buddy Rich, Louis Belson, and already his great hero, Gene Krupa. Add to this confluence of coincidence, our new drinking mate, Harry Kings, who was already wowing the Labour Club pre-bingo assembly, every Wednesday night with some solo guitar recitals, and Terry Imms, who kept him good musical company on bass, and you can see the stirrings of an idea beginning in Martin's vivid, but usually unproductive mind.

We arranged to meet in the Golden Lion. Everybody was excited, we had two guitarists, a drummer, and a sax player. Mick could actually play the piano, in very passable boogie style, but he decided it would be a bastard trying to take it on the bus. My part in these orchestral manoeuvres on the piss, was to organise the scout hut as a practice room (being an ex cub in 'stoat patrol' or whatever) and I duly convinced our 'skip' he was doing a noble community a stirring service. I'd also discovered I had a certain second-rate flair on the 'skins' and used to crash around on Martin's Speedfire set, when the mood took me, and when Mart's wrists seized up. We began to practice regularly, Mick and Terry shared the main vocals and I joined in with the harmony stuff, and did the odd Clyde McPhatter impersonation. He was a unique and wonderful talent and I wasn't, but my renditions always caused our audiences to sit up and take notice, in fact, quite often it caused them to stand up and leave the auditorium. Mick said I did to Clyde what John Profumo did to Christine Keeler, but when he did it, he kept his mouth shut.

So the 1st Bromsgrove Scout hut became our Cavern Club and night after night we were tortured by our art. We called ourselves Gezenstax, Martin thought it up and said it was from an old German word for a warlock, and combined with the great American jazz label, made a clever word association mental picture. In all the time we were together, nobody ever understood what it was all about. How clever was that?

We practiced and practiced, the guitars sounded really good and Mick filled in with everything on the alto, and even better on the piano. Mart was demonically animated and really fortissimo; that's Italian for very fucking loud. The scout master liked it, and courtesy of one of his mates, got the band a couple of pub bookings.

Britain ruled the world of popular music and the Mersey beat ruled Britain. American stars and groups, were blown away, even the heroes of rock n' roll had to take a back seat, whilst the Beatles, Gerry, the Searchers and any other band that knew where the pierhead was, filled the charts with home grown sounds. It was a genuine phenomena, and spread throughout the country. Every town and village produced a competent band, the hills indeed, were alive with the sound of music. The bookings continued to come in, we added Bruce Chanel, Tommy Roe, the Clovers, the Isley Brothers' and other defining numbers to our repertoire, it was rope for old money. The film 'Drum Crazy' was released and starred Sal Mineo as Gene Krupa, although Gene was still alive and playing. Martin and I went to see it together, then, he went another twenty times to see it on his own. We kept practicing and we got better. Martin got louder, but better. The film really inspired him and my 'cover' gigs became less and less.

We played alongside the Rockin' Berries at Rubery Social (I'm really name dropping now), Carl Wayne, of later 'Move' fame, and his Vikings, at Tardebigge club, and our moment of supreme triumph, as a warm-up act to Gerry and the Pacemakers at Droitwich Winter Gardens.

In those days the 'fee' was about fifteen pounds for the whole band and all the beer you could drink, for free. The compere introduced us as Guys and Stocks, or some-such, and we tore through our entire set in an alcoholic trance.

We got to meet Gerry backstage, a pleasant scouse mouse, who was destined to become the first artist to record three consecutive number one hits in the British charts, and to be forever associated with Liverpool

Football Club, with his anthem 'You'll Never Walk Alone'.

We packed up our kit, Harry fell off the stage and bent Martin's high-hat cymbal, the taxi wouldn't drive us back to Worcester, and we slept in the group van, until Terry was sober enough to get us to our homes. 'You'll Never Walk Back Home'.

We did a few south Birmingham social clubs and pubs, and rubbed shoulders with Roy Wood, Jasper Carrott, and other fledgling brummie superstars. Harry went off to join the Playboys, as regular house band at the Chalet Club, in Rednal, and we folded up our tents and left the music scene to more talented performers.

It was a good time to be alive, we had some wild nights and met some very interesting people. I developed a lifelong penchant for Chablis, learnt how to smoke pot without laughing, and managed to come through a period of wearing absurd clothes without lasting damage.

A high school classmate, Euan Rose, had a top twenty hit with his group 'The Cheetahs', and were resident band for a couple of years at the Imperial Hotel in Birmingham. He went on to manage the Alex Theatre.

I can honestly say fame never changed me; I'm glad Clyde McPhatter never heard me.

We all went our different ways after the band era, and I gradually lost touch with all the lads. My last contact with Martin was in 1967, when I was about to get married. His own marriage had foundered a couple of years earlier and he'd moved to Isleworth in Middlesex. He lived in a flat just off the main commuter road between Slough and Uxbridge. There was, and still is, a very large Indian and Pakistani population in that part of London. The locals used to call the road the Khyber Pass.

I went down by train to see him, we visited Windsor and had a pleasant meal in the lovely garden of a rather top-hole restaurant. Martin didn't say what he was doing, but obviously he was ok for cash and seemed happy and contented. The marriage had never stood a chance, and he was relieved to be away from Bromsgrove and all the chit-chat.

Back at his flat, we sat and had a few drinks and he generously gave me two tickets for a concert at the Albert Hall, featuring the Red Army choir. It was his wedding present. He'd built up a fabulous LP collection, all classical, lots of Mozart, Brahms, Haydn and a burgeoning number of opera recordings.

We were listening to 'The Magic Flute', I think, when he produced an American import copy of 'Skin Deep' by Louis Belson, the great drummer, one time with Duke Ellington's mighty orchestra. He said 'please keep it, to remind you of the old times'.

Whilst he was shuffling through the record collection, I fleetingly noticed 'Drum Crazy'.

Some things you just can't let go.

CHAPTER ELEVEN

The Pirates Favourite Letter

Bert Nicholls came to work for Neath Brothers Removals and in an inspired moment, my dad put me to work with him. We were soul brothers from the start:
"There is a pleasure sure
In being mad, which none but madmen know!"
Bert was a small wiry man, but fit and surprisingly powerful. Two big ticks in the right boxes, considering all the first-floor bound piano's that were waiting in the house mover's future for us both. He was a natural wit, told an interesting tale in an engaging Herefordshire accent, was eternally cheerful, enjoyed a few beers after work and was semi-demented.

We got on like a pantechnicon on fire. Bert's home was the village of Wellington Heath in the Marches country, where apples grew on trees. His family had its roots in South Wales, as indeed did mine, so whilst not on the scale of the Jewish diaspora, our displacement acted as a catalyst to our friendship.

We very soon became the 'A' team, in this case, the 'away' from home team, as my dad quickly realised he had found the solution to the thorny problem of calling on a crew that would do the long hauls, often at weekends, that involved nights' out and unsociable hours.

Bert was going through a nasty divorce that was becoming ever nastier, courtesy of the legal profession. As Wodehouse would have it 'In the matter of divorce, lawyers display that reckless generosity, which is found only in men who are giving away someone else's money'.

With my own nemesis, in this condition, as yet merely a twinkle in an unknown judge's eye, we were both, if not completely fancy free, at least footloose and available for travel and sojourn in faraway places.

With my mother and Bert's wife, mercifully freed from providing shelter for us both, the nesting instinct raised its unexpected head. We converted the front over-cab area of the van, known as the 'Luton', since the first examples of its type were built in that town, into our over-night accommodation. 'Cab Hotel' was to be our postcard address for many nights in the next twelve months.

With a mattress and bedding, water flask, bowl, soap and shaving kit, the van was considerably better appointed, not to mention cleaner, than the vast majority of drivers' bed and breakfast dens, the length and breadth of the country in those pre-corporate truck-stop days.

An added bonus was the saving of said expenses on overnight luxury stops at "Chez Cockroach" in Shepherds Bush and the like, enabling us to hit the clubs, at least any of them that took the C.I.U. card, and drink the night away over the snooker table.

Mentioning Shepherds Bush, reminds me of 'Corsini's', a desperate B and B, where you picked up the key from his café in Goldhawk Road and let yourself into, and out of, the 'barracks' about three streets away. By returning the key the next morning, you qualified for breakfast.

The first night we stopped there, we returned to the dormitory after a night round the local pubs, to find our beds surrounded by a barrier of Guinness bottles and occupied by two huge, snoring, fully dressed Irish Navvies. "Who's going to wake 'em up, your or me?" said Bert. I think it was that night on the floor that really made up our minds to go 'mobile'.

A good nights' sleep is never having to have your lights punched out by a drunken, Irish, Shrek look-alike. So out came the Slumberland, on went the nightgown and tasselled, pointed cap, off flicked the torch and hey-ho, we were dreaming the life.

'If you can't get digs, get pissed', the drivers code. That 'Car Parks of Great Britain' guide book was just waiting for me to write it.

There were drawbacks. When the vehicle was really fully loaded, it was difficult to leave a 'path' from the back to the bedroom area at the front. I've spent some nights hard against the roof, and woke up with my mouth stuck to the boards.

Particularly memorable was a freezing night in Lincoln, with six inches of snow on the ground. With the vehicle packed solid, we spent the night in deckchairs, with the tailboard half open. I dressed for the night in all my clothes, jeans, pullover, duffel coat, woolly hat and Wellington boots. Bert then covered me with layers of Hessian that we used as packing material. Fully dressed also, he pulled another pile of packing onto himself, and amazingly we somehow fell into a shivering sleep.

Rosy fingered dawn came up, not over Homer's olive groves, but Lincoln municipal car park. The Cathedral bells pealed out the time, seven o'clock and all was not bloody well. Christ, I'd lost the use of my legs; panic over, my fucking Wellingtons were frozen to the floor-boards. Panic on again, I couldn't move my arms, the hessian had formed an icy cocoon and the snow was still falling. I looked and felt like a cold, hard boiled egg.

Barely able to turn my head, I caught sight of Bert and a strangled cry escaped my lips. He was reclining in the deckchair and covered in a fine layer of shining snow. He'd not put his hood up and his hair and eyebrows were completely white with frost.

I imagined that's how Captain Scott and his brave men must have looked, when they first pulled open the tent, on that ill-fated expedition.

Nearly hysterical, I could see no movement. "Bert are you alive?" stupid question. A twitch of the nose, an eye opened, there was a mini-avalanche from the hair and eyebrows. "The central heating's bollocksed again". Relief, then a titanic struggle ensued as we both strove to move the crushing hessian. Finally the frozen mass relinquished its grip and we heaved it onto the floor.

I sucked my feet from the wellingtons and freed them from the floor-boards with a handy garden spade. We both stood and looked at each other. Snow-sparkling hair, black streaked faces, wild eyed and filthy, clothes like rags, breath like satan. Just another night in Cab Hotel.

We climbed out onto the snowy carpet, locked up the tail-board and clumped off to find a greasy spoon. Another escape from an icy death for two of Bromsgrove's finest.

Now I don't want to give the wrong impression, not all of our trips were like that one; some were much, much worse, but perhaps not so much fun. One that was however, occurred not in East Anglia, but my own favourite West Country. We were bucketing down to Brixham on a summer Sunday afternoon, the sun was up, Bert was mad, we had diesel in the tank, Senior Service in their packets, money in our pocket, an easy drive, and a free night out ahead of us.

Bert was giving the girls the eye and his Leslie Phillips greeting, as we rolled through the A38 towns on the great road to the west. Between cigarettes, we played the battle of the worst ever pop songs, each singing as much as we knew of the most despicable tunes ever to reach the charts. Bert won this contest with an awfully accurate rendition of David Such's 'I put a spell on you'. I made a winners' banner and pinned it to the back of the cab. It read "Bert Ding Dong Screaming Lord Nicholls'.

On our way through Devon we banged the cab doors and Bert blew the horn as we passed through Ashburton, headquarters of the Raving Looney Party. I believe the party even got members elected onto the local council. Devon's got to be a really good place to live.

Eventually, we pitched up in Brixham, to be the venue of our 'Francis Drake Impression' night. Drake was a Devonian and our tribute to this great British seaman came fittingly in the fishing port of Brixham. Drake and Raleigh, he of potato and tobacco fame, were contemporaries in the second half of the sixteenth century, but whilst Francis was always a favourite at court, Walter eventually came unstuck, when he went loco up the Orinoco and found himself up the creek, not without a paddle, but his head. Political scheming in those days could certainly reward a real go-getter with a mansion or two and half an English county to call his back garden, but the margin of error in the sycophant stakes was extremely fine, just as was the executioner's blade.

So here we were on yet another Sunday night away from home, strolling through the town on a balmy summer's evening, with the smell of mackerel, not beef-burgers, permeating the air. Brixham still had a busy, working, fishing industry in those days, and the quayside market still held its daily auctions, providing fish and crustaceans for the domestic tables, fish shops and restaurants of south Devon, not the tapas bars of Spain. The local council had not yet sold its soul to the 'holiday entrepreneurs', who turned all Britains seaside towns into basic 'ABC' resorts; arcades, boutiques and chip shops. These vandals would have opened 'McDonalds' and an off-licence in the garden of Eden.

After a 'recce' of the harbour pubs, we fetched up in the London Inn. It was a bright, unpretentious, cheerful pub, full of locals, happily reducing the landlords stocks of Courage beers. They were good Devonian drinking men, who obviously stood by the principle that it was wicked to stand idly by and let the beer go bad.

The door to the bar stood ajar and the salted scent of the sea wafted into the room, as the falling tide lapped gently against the bobbing fishing boats. The light was fading, yellow lamps began to cast their shadows on the harbour wall, and from a café across the street Sonny and Cher sang of their undying love 'I Got you Babe'.

I was slipping into a reverie; the 'Courage' was taking its toll. We were in the 'Admiral Benbow', a tall man with a wooden leg stood at the bar, in the corner a blind sailor was passing a note to a surprised fellow drinker; he unfolded the piece of paper to find a large black spot, nothing else. From another room in the house came the chorus of lament "Fifteen men on a dead man's chest......"

Bloody hell, this 'Special Directors' was a bit tasty, better get a breath of fresh air. Bert and I stumbled out onto the quayside and draping ourselves over the safety railings, looked out across Torbay, where the black Devon night cascaded its million silver stars into the blacker English Channel. Silence hung like a heavy curtain.

"How beautiful is night.

A dewy freshness fills the silent air;"

Zeus, the ruler of the gods, when he tired of being omnipotent, used to indulge himself in sexual peccadillo's; sometimes making love to animals and birds, sometimes in animal form himself. Whilst not for a moment suggesting that any of our tribe were in any way or form deities, I have to wonder whether perhaps, a magpie once got in amongst us, in a manner of speaking.

I have always been a collector. Stamps, stones from the beach, match boxes, horrifically, for a few weeks, leeches from the brook, bubble-gum cards, American comics, train numbers, then as my interests changed, beer mats, ashtrays and hangovers.

Before I departed from the 'London Inn' I asked the landlord if I might purchase a natty, three-cornered, heavy porcelain item, extolling the virtues of some lager or other. He said as I'd drunk ten pints, I already had bought it. I clutched it tightly as we weaved along the inner harbour wall, on our way back to the vehicle park.

It was then, as we turned the corner, we saw her, in all her maritime glory: 'The Golden Hind'.

She was an awe-inspiring sight, pennants flying from her mast-heads, canon 'ready for action' at their gun-ports, as she dipped and rolled at her mooring on the slowly ebbing tide.

Drake had taken her round the world in 1577, 'circumcised it' Bert said. We too were sons of Albion, salt and beer ran in our veins, the sea was in our history and in the very air we breathed. We heard the drum a 'beatin' Yes! "We'd drum 'em up the Channel, as we drummed then long ago". Our ambition was somewhat smaller, but nonetheless laudable; we decided to sail her to Torquay.

Our Courage was high, ten pints high, as we clambered aboard. Curses vent the night air, as we stumbled over ropes and sheets, kicking canon-ball stacks along the deck like giant ten-pin balls. Apart from all this expletive-laden commotion, all decent Devon people were taking to their beds. I stowed my prize ashtray in the wheelhouse and looking seaward, marvelled at the astral tapestry of the night. Bert was shivering his timbers, belaying spectral matey's and holding a truncated conversation with a non-existent parrot. With 'rrr's' and 'Jim lads' punctuating every sentence, he was fast descending into a Long John Silver state of mind.

Joining in the nautical banter, I returned to the quay to find the ship secured to four capstans, handily sited next to the 'Hind', I remember thinking.

It was a difficult job to release her from the expertly knotted cables, but I worked diligently and eventually made a decent fist of slacking the ropes in unison, and hurling them onboard, without the vessel taking to the high seas without half her crew. With only the moonlight and the anaesthetic properties of 5% proof best bitter to assist and comfort me, I managed to cast off, with no loss of fingers, only cosmetic nail damage and third degree burns from the coarse, bitumen treated sisal ropes.

Meanwhile onboard, the sound of iron on timber announced Bert's success in rolling out the guns on the seaward side of the ship. The adrenalin ran high and was about to run higher, as Bert began to ascend the rigging to the crows nest. With the full moon behind him, he cut a fine figure of a naval man, swaying across the deck some thirty or more feet in the air. Only a cutlass gripped in his teeth, could have improved this growling, cursing, moonlight-serenading, piratical cameo.

It was whilst marvelling at this acrobatic tour de force, that two things, almost simultaneously, occurred to me.

Firstly, although we were no longer secured in our moorings, I had no idea how we might actually get under way. My sea-faring expertise up to this point, consisted almost in total, in being able to get on and off the 'Severn Belle', before and after a so-called Jazz Cruise, and not fall into the Severn, at Worcester.

Secondly, and certainly somewhat more disconcerting, not to say disorientating, was the slow dawning awareness that my sight-line had shifted from the quayside to the roof of the fish-market.

Never one slow to grasp the full import of an extraordinary situation, I shouted to Bert "Quick, look, the fish market's collapsing".

"No its not, you prat, the fucking ship's capsizing!"

It was only now, fully assimilating the wisdom of Bert's utterance, that our plight became apparent. Holding on to the deck-rail for dear life, I peered over the side and to my horror, found that the tide had gone out. We were grounded and keeling over at about forty five degrees. Thank God for mud.

The Golden Hind had settled in about six feet of the foul smelling harbour silt. As we struggled to marshal our thoughts on what next to do, two of the harbour-side canon ran backwards across the deck and smashed through the gun ports on the opposite side, disappearing from sight into the evil quagmire. A torrent of unholy invective poured from above and I dimly discerned Bert's spread-eagled form, dark and tarantula like, clinging at a dizzying angle to the rigging.

A beam of light sliced through this dark, demonic tapestry; the voice of sanity, of authority, of the South Devon Constabulary: "And what do you think you're playing at, Captain fucking Bligh?" Obviously the local police training centre imbues its members with a rapier sense of humour, and not to be dismissed ability to summarise and defuse a potentially critical situation.

'Captain Bligh' gingerly descended and we both, embarrassingly, walked the gangplank to land thankfully, on dry Devon land.

The cell in Brixham police station, whilst not over-cosy, was warm and reassuringly level, and they let us stay together overnight.

The morning brought us tea and biscuits, but amazingly, no charges. I think this may have been because, as we walked back to our vehicle in the car park, we spied the 'Golden Hind' proud and upright at her moorings, looking none the worse for our nocturnal occupation. They obviously hadn't counted her guns though, so Bert fired up the motor and we hot-footed it, out of Brixham and back to the sea-free sanctuary of Worcestershire. I never even went back for the ashtray.

Oh, and the pirates' favourite letter? 'R' of course.

CHAPTER TWELVE

A Major Coup

Although we had been banned from Perry Hall by the Menorcan Melon vendor, we continued to sneak back every second Monday for 'Jazz Club'. 'The Canteloope Kid' used to take these evenings off and nobody else at Perry Hall was interested in keeping us out.

It was a very popular venue in the town and long before the music began, the place was densely packed. I mean by this, it was packed with dense people.

'Trad' jazz was enjoying a renaissance, and bands like Acker Bilk and Kenny Ball, jumped eagerly on the New Orleans bandwagon. Arguments raged as to whether Acker was better than Louis Armstrong, and Kenny could outplay Sidney Bechet; as I mentioned, the place was rammed with musical morons.

The boom only lasted about a year, then market forces came strongly into play, and modern 'pop' took over the evenings. It was the age of new youthful exuberance and expression, or as the guardians of Britain's spiritual well-being preferred to call it, moral turpitude.

I lived in high anxiety through the period of sex, drugs and rock and roll. I never seemed to be in possession of enough of the first part, decided not to use too much of the second part, and told outrageous stories about my experiences in the third part, mainly to improve my chances in the first part.

One night in the smoke filled enclave of the club, where by about eleven o'clock, you felt as though you were taking a sauna, with all your clothes on, in the drying house of a mackerel shed, a typical scene unfolded:

Fired up by cousin John's 100% proof Navy Rum, motto: 'A wee drappie makes your guts gangle all agley', (This was obviously the Scottish navy), young rock n' roll devotees, sat at the foot of the master, me, as I signed copies of our latest chart success 'Louie Louie'.

I had managed to convince them, that the boys and I were the group 'The Kingsmen', at that time number one on the Billboard hot hundred in America. With an accent ranging, due to the ravages of drink, from Tennessee hillbilly to Boston drawl, I painted an improbable and wholly fictitious picture of our struggle for recognition, years of frustration, and finally, glorious success in the wicked world of 'pop'. This was an oft-used ploy and with luck, would lead to a walking home routine, with one of the female fans. That's if any of us could manage the walking bit.

Bromsgrove used to be such a pleasant, welcoming, friendly little town, inhabited by simple, trusting descendants of forthright yeoman stock, and public and grammar school educated lying bastards. Everyone knew their place back then, but half of them wanted it to be somewhere else.

It was on one such sultry evening in the 1967 summer of love, running the gauntlet of passive Senior Service inhalation, and the heady cocktail of 'cuba libre' and testosterone, there appeared Judy and Liz, the sisters' Major. If that makes them sound like a small constellation, they certainly had a stellar effect on Colin and Ernie, respectively.

To complete a natural progression, with Scott Mckenzie going to San Francisco, the Bee Gees to Massachusetts, Colin and Ernie decided to go to a house on the canal-side in Tardebigge. They were smitten, the dye was cast; all they needed to do was fall down in a bakery, and they could truly wear some flour in their hair.

We were about to lose two of our drinking mates; Sunday mornings waking up with Ernie's frying pan stuck to the side of your face, sodden papier-mâché in your trouser back-pocket, where your money used to be, the cigarette-scented breath of an unknown woman, in a deep, heaving sleep, ruffling your hair, as you both fitted, like contortionists, into a two-seater settee. But on the plus side, we were also about to enter the wonderful world of Dougie and Dorothy.

They were the parents of the girls and they all lived in an eloquently crumbling Georgian house, standing aloof in its own grounds, near the Worcester and Birmingham canal, at the point where the famous 'Hopwood Lift' raised the 'cut' over the Lickey Hills, by means of thirty one daunting locks.

Dougie was a brewery solicitor, who brought most of his work home with him. That was the brewery half. Dorothy was a retired music teacher and an exceptional classical pianist. She was a bohemian, with an unusual dress sense, and shared Dougie's interest in the brewery aspect of the law. She was definitely more Chopin than Shopping.

Both Oxford graduates, old money, old school, upper crust, but from a generous, natural, warm-hearted loaf, and the most monumental topers.

Dougie had a wine cellar of epic proportions and we all took great delight in receiving practical instruction in all aspects of the vintners craft.

To stay for a drink with Doug and Dorothy was to guarantee a night wrapped in the blanket of oblivion. People would arrive at various times, seemingly all through the night; newcomers would wrest the half-full bottles from the grip of the fallen, already embraced by morpheus. The bacchanalian relay would continue until the dawn, or merciful slumber, engulfed the drowsy company.

By a great irresponsible coincidence, an original canal engine house nearby, had been converted into an exclusive night spot, owned by the Jazz singer Marion Montgomery and her husband Lawrie Holloway. Dougie knew them both well and we were able to spend many evenings in the intimate little club, where cool music, often with Marion herself singing, and a seemingly endless supply of champagne and fine wines, made Bromsgrove, only three miles distant, seem light years away.

Then, with the beautifully haunting melody of Cole Porters 'Every time we say goodbye', resonant under the starry sky, we meandered waist-high through the ghostly yellow corn fields, back to the house.

Whilst Dougie repaired to the cellar, for the milliners' shopful of night-caps, and Dorothy busied herself in the kitchen with sandwiches and the like, we set to work with the minor Major's, to clear the huge drawing room of various chairs, settees, sofas and other furniture, in preparation for the musical soiree that was to follow. With her drink on a small table, thoughtfully placed close at hand, Dorothy began to play the Bechstein full concert grand piano. The limpid, transparent, singing melodies of Chopin were her forte, and the recital would take us through to the Ballades, preludes and etudes of that most wistful and emotionally expressive composer.

With the room now lit with only small, clustered wall-lights, and the three great sash windows, each one over ten feet high and six feet wide, fully opened, the intoxicating night scent of honeysuckle and rhododendron wafted in through the room, while the timeless music floated out, bathing in the perfume of the yellow-moon night.

Drinking and sinking into easy-wrapping cushions, I see it and hear it still, an unforgettable cameo, that from the very first time, stirs me always; indeed, like Robert Browning's 'First fine careless rapture', there is no possibility that I never will recapture it.

Applause, ovation, for this Polish sensation. Now for the dancing.

On with the record player, music from the shows; Dorothy and the girls, lady friends we'd coaxed back from the club, the band struck up, all of us swirling, girling, revelling and bedevilling. A full measure of chaos, until the whole room was awash with South Pacific. We scythed through Oklahoma and met Pal Joey, spinning on the carousel. Gershwin and Hammerstein, Berlin and Hart; masters of their craft, legends in their own lithe times. How subtle and versatile, they would go on to form the defensive heart of Germany's World Cup winning football team of 1954.

It was on such a night in this conservative conservatoire, at the height of a frantic fandango, another image flickers into the magic lantern of my minds eye.

As the candle lights gutter on the pianos candelabra, Dorothy and 'Slicker' cut a swathe through the lesser tripsters, casting an umbrella of perspiration across the floor, roaring, ever faster, spinning like dervishes. Centre floor, side to side, round again, then, with a final flourish, like a dismissive matador discarding his cape, he cast her from him, and following a wild gyration across the room, she tripped on the window sill, only a foot from the floor and disappeared through the gaping frame into the night.

Great entrances there have been many, but never surely a greater exit than this.

The party nights were legendary. There was nothing remotely like a quiet night at Dougies. They could have sold tickets. So much warmth and happiness, squeezed from the orange of goodness, into one small candle-lit room in the crowding darkness of a Worcestershire summer night.

Then, at what turned out to be one of the last of these gatherings, both Colin and Ernie announced their engagements to the Major girls. Tears of happiness, advice, consolation, (playful smacks in the mouth), congratulations, salutations, much hand shaking, kissing and backslapping ensued. Some of us even spoke to the blokes.

Then a little celebratory drink, which even by the two 'D's standards, went off the Richter and into the epic scale.

Plans were set in motion for the weddings.

CHAPTER THIRTEEN

Wellington Meets his Waterloo

It was six thirty on Saturday night, I found Colin alone in the lounge of Perry Hall. He was alone because nobody was with him at his table and nobody else was in the room.

The Spanish fruit-flogger had relented and let us all back into the hotel. I think he missed the sixty or seventy pints we used to get through each session and looking around me, I was sure I was right.

Tonight however, the table décor was a little different. A bottle of Smirnoff Vodka sat in the centre and two large tonics nestled in an ice-bucket. Two glasses completed the line-up and I was pleased to discover one of them was for me. All of this was unusual. Also, Colin was drunk, had a six inch cigar in his mouth and a silly, sideways grin on his face. Oh and he was sat on his Russian hat.

This was very unusual. Colin didn't smoke.

'I've got some good news' he slurred. I said I knew he was marrying a lovely girl and I congratulated him on stealing a bottle of Vodka. 'No, not that, we've got some money'.

As I pondered whether I could cram a couple of vodka tonics down me before the police arrived, he began to enlighten me.

We'd all been in the Golden Lion the night before and Jack, he of the 'Sporting Life' and the flawed footwear, had been in full cry. It was the 'Oaks' on Saturday and Jack had had a vision. He'd been on the scotch, it could well have been a double vision.

His dear, departed, much loved mom, had appeared before him and told him to put all his money, and both his sole-less shoes, on a horse with a name that conjured up a happy event. That was typical of Jack's racing information, it was never cut and dried, you always had to work out some sort of enigmatic puzzle. Even his dead relatives wouldn't give him the horses fucking name.

The vodka found its mark, I struggled to find the answer, then, of course, the whole pub had worked it out, 'Wedding Bells'. How could it be anything else? Something niggled, I didn't think it was right.

Colin slumped back in his seat, an angelic rictus smile on his face. 'I don't think wedding bells is necessarily the portend of a happy event', he offered, rather ungallantly I thought, for a man engaged to be married just a week away. "Do you remember lying on the floor, looking at the holes in Jack's shoes, saying it's a good job he hasn't got far to go, to get his head down?' I couldn't; so what, what was the point of this vodka fuelled nonsense conversation?

"I had a look in the paper this morning, and thinking of Jack, and his dead mom, I put a fiver on 'Homeward Bound'. It won at 33/1."

He told me I was the inspiration for his bet and counted out eighty two pounds, ten shillings, onto the table. I know this doesn't sound such a big deal now, but back then I was working about seventy hours a week for my dad and took home about fifteen pounds for my pains. I had five and half week's wages on the table; it was going to be a very long night.

The gang drifted in, more bottles were ordered, the abandon became truly gay. By ten o'clock Colin was speaking in tongues, none of them English. He told us the wedding plans, everybody nodded agreement; we couldn't speak. We were all spellbound by the wonder of the moment, nobody left, we couldn't stand.

If paramedics had been invented then, they would have definitely been summoned. We were paralytic.

I was to be best man at Colin's wedding. He warned me to change the habits of a lifetime and not turn up pissed for his big day. It was only because he didn't want me to have a head-start. 'Homeward Bound' gave me a seven day headache, what sort of happy event was that?

The wedding day dawned, I got a taxi to Judy's house and all the guests were gathering, splitting off, amoeba like, into little factions, nuptially nattering.

It was a formal do, grey penguin suits, and glory be, the reception was at A.E. Housman's old pad. God, I thought, best man to my dearest friend, in the old Jazz Club room, scene of so many raucous, raging nights of indecent lust, lies and debauchery; now the setting for Dougie and Dorothy to give away their daughter, amidst their closest friends and business colleagues, many of whom I'd met at the house parties.

No change there then, I thought. My other thought was, Tony's about to take a fortnights turnover in one afternoon.

I was at my 'meet and greet' station at the door and scanned the room, as the people began to arrive. Judy looked radiant, Colin looked lucky, all the gang looked sober, Dougie looked noble and Dorothy looked like Henry Cooper. She had a magnificent black eye and standing adjacent to me at the door, resembled a photo-negative panda.

I caught myself staring at her, wondering if Dougie had 'clocked' her the night before, for playing a bum note, when she turned to me, spookily reading my thoughts; "Bruce darling, what beastly bad luck. I walked into that fucking revolving door into our kitchen again, last night. My timing as ever, is immaculate." There wasn't a revolving door into her kitchen and whatever she walked into, I've no idea, but she was burning like a super-nova that day, and pride incinerated prejudice before it left the launching pad.

She was tempestuous and full of inner fire. It was her day and Judy's day. Bugger the guests and protocol. The mistress of Chopin in the house of the Shropshire Lad: "Clay lies still, but blood's a rover."

I welcomed and announced the guests. There were hundreds of them. Dorothy's academic friends, the girls 'uni' gang, Colin's mates and partners, and outnumbering them all, Dougie's friends and associates from M and B, and the legal profession. It occurred to me, we were organising a brewery in a piss-up.

The tired old Jazz Club room had washed her face, combed her hair, brushed her teeth and put on her best summer dress. The late afternoon sun slanted in off the Malverns, the wine began to saturate the vital organs, a pleasing numbness visited the head and the time arrived for the speeches.

The top table was a 'Bollinger' bottle battlefield. With a calmness born in desperation, I cleared a path through silica valley, begged the silence of the host and introduced Dorothy.

Emotion had clearly consumed her and her pride in her daughter was evident. Colin and Dorothy had rubbed along famously from their very first meeting, and the match received her whole-hearted blessing.

With some difficulty she got to her feet and spreading her palms on the table top, surveyed the crowded room. She was a small woman and barely managed to rise above the bottle collection laid out before her, but she was not to be denied her moment. She fixed the assembly with eyes blazing with fulfilment, the left one particularly striking, surrounded by its black and purple aureole. With an open-handed acknowledgement to the happy couple, she delivered the shortest and most amazing wedding speech any of the assembled throng had ever heard. It is etched in my memory and I'm sure, in the folklore of Bromsgrove.

"I think it was the Duke of Wellington who said, 'If you've got anything to say, stand up, say it, then sit down and shut up.' So I've stood up, said it, now I'm going to sit down and shut up."

With one final acknowledgement to the guests and to the couple, she haltingly regained the sitting position, then, with a smile of glorious contentment, she slid off the chair and under the table.

There was deafening applause. Everyone rose to their feet for a standing ovation. It could only have been topped with a Mexican wave.

Two ushers arrived and helped me redeem her from the floor. The band struck up and Roy the milkman sand 'All the Way' in pretty fine Sinatra style.

Music filled the air, everyone grabbed someone and staggered happily round the dance floor in an après-champers dance facsimile; some of them even managed to stay upright.

Colin and Judy changed into twentieth century clothes, and after a short speech of thanks, we bade them farewell and good luck.

As we shouted our good-byes to the disappearing bridal car, the clanking cans in its wake signalled the end of the Perry Hall poet society.

Ernie and Liz were married a month later, and became licensees of a pub in Redditch. Mr. and Mrs. Gamekeeper nee Poacher.

We still all met of course, but it was with decreasing frequency, and we diminishing members of unmarried blokes continued to stumble up and down the High street on the raffle run.

It was bloody hard to swallow, but we grudgingly had to admit it, we were all growing up.

CHAPTER FOURTEEN

Ar Hyd Y Nos

A quartet of mature men formed a half circle around a pole-supported, swaying lantern. Each held a small book of carols in mittened hands.

They all wore full dinner suits with crisp white dress-shirts and black bow ties. Dark heavy top-coats protected them from the elements, and white silk scarves and shining top-hats completed the elegant ensemble. One of them sported a fine ebony walking stick, topped with an onyx orb held in a silver crown-shaped clasp.

Snow was falling, but gently. The lantern's light danced around their faces, the starry flakes settled on their shoulders and they began the first song.

The men sang lustily in two part harmony and the sounds were carried away to the heavens, in the quiet, snow-muffled street. Their last offering to the programme was always 'All through the Night'. The chorister with the ebony cane always began and took the first verse alone, but in Welsh, 'Ar Hyd Y Nos'.

He was my father, Percy James Neath.

It was ever thus for many Christmas Eve's, not in some high eisteddfod, but the courtyards and beer gardens of the pubs of Bromsgrove, always beginning at the steps of the Britannia Inn, my father's, and the other members, favourite local.

The object of this annual Christmas festival, apart from realising the twin ambitions of dressing in all their finery, and singing, without interruption to a grateful and receptive audience, was to raise money for Bromsgrove's Cottage Hospital.

The sponsors were not the local rotary, but the Britannia Duck Club, perhaps a little less noble, but certainly no less munificent.

The club was run from the pub, by a hierarchy more secretive than the Cosa Nostra. It was said that anyone could join, but only if the existing members wanted them to. It therefore required careful and continuous lobbying to gain their favour, except of course, that you didn't know who they were.

Joseph Heller must have drunk in the 'Brit' in an earlier life and gained his inspiration for 'Catch 22'.

Whilst I mustn't dwell on this institution, nor give away any more of its secrets, it may exist still, I think it fair to describe the initiation ceremony as a combination of the Masonic (allegedly) and the Kama Sutra.

Suffice to say, that on my own induction evening, after becoming intimately involved with several different fruits, my genitals were subjected to numerous encounters with what felt like tepid custard, and once, possibly, a snake's mouth.

But it was all in a good cause and for a small club they raised incredible sums of money throughout the year, with high-flown and even lunatic schemes. With some pride and a recurrent fear, that visits me still on occasions, I remember the highlight of my own fund-raising.

During one alcohol-fuelled general meeting, I agreed to do a parachute jump at Bidford on Avon airfield. I accompanied by friend and fellow Duck Club member, Ron Thomas, to undergo my period of intensive training for this death-defying event. At least, I kept telling myself it would be death-defying.

The training consisted of one winch-lifted flight in a Cessna light aircraft, and jumping off a two-foot wall shouting "One thousand, two thousand." With this regime completed, Ron assured me I was now fully competent and ready for the jump.

So, cometh the day, cometh the terrified man. After the confidence boosting ceremony, of signing the death indemnity form, away to the bright blue yonder I went, leaving my stomach and most of my nerve-endings on the runway. Jumping out on the running-line, I shouted the famous training mantra, and thank God in his Heaven, the parachute opened. Seconds later, as I was beginning to half enjoy the experience, I was approaching the ground at what seemed to be excessive speed. Remembering the 'tuck up and roll over' instructions, I put this into operation and all went according to the manual. Except, that is, I had overshot the landing area by a few yards and came down in a field full of sprout plants.

I had never considered a sprout to be a dangerous weapon before, but that was prior to finding one attempting to enter my bottom at about twenty miles an hour.

It occurred to me that the Duck Club's function, certainly in my case, up til now, had been to assault my private parts with fruit and vegetables.

We all carried a small yellow plastic duck about our person, as they say, and if challenged at any time and in any place, by a fellow member, failure to show one's duck resulted in a fine, to be paid into the hospital fund. These challenges could occur at the most inconvenient time, like in the swimming baths, or the public lavatory, and suffice to say, considerable sums were forthcoming, purely due to impracticality or forgetfulness. The club therefore created the concept of fund raising by amnesia.

My years of membership of this barmy society were full of hare-brained schemes and madcap ideas, but all in the most deserving cause. The Bromsgrove Duck Club can be proud of its existence.

Today the Britannia pub is a solicitor's office, so no more charity there, and the old Cottage Hospital has been demolished to make way for a shopping centre. That's just what the nation needs, more lawyers and supermarkets.

My earliest memory of a family holiday was a visit to Clevedon, in Somerset. Dad hadn't got a car, but borrowed one from a friend. I'm sure it was a Triumph Mayflower saloon, a large 'sit up and beg' machine complete with proper 'dicky' boot and white-wall tyres.

The old girl was no flying machine and memory tells me it took about half a day to get down there. Clevedon is understated and sophisticated. It's Weston-Super-Mare-s elderly aunt. Clevedon's tea and scones, Weston's lager and chips. Clevedon has a Victorian pier with wrought iron framework and an open promenade. Weston has a quarter-mile long arcade and candy floss.

That few miles along the Bristol Channel provides an altogether more refined experience. I don't actually think Dad picked it because of that, more likely it was to save another half day's driving. Strangely, I can't remember doing anything together as a family in Clevedon. Mind you, I've been back since and apart from bowling, there's still nothing to do.

Later, we safari'd down to glorious Devon and Mrs. Heath's guesthouse in Brixham. She had the most wonderful accent and I hear her now, "Do'ee want a cup o'char?" It was here that a pattern for the future began to emerge. Dad would drive us down, stay with us for a couple of days, then away back to Bromsgrove and the never ending demands of Neath Bros.

A tableau, still fresh in my mind; my mother, my sister and me, all clambering aboard the 'Western Lady', the steamer that crossed Torbay to Torquay, every day of the season. It was early evening, the lights beginning to twinkle all over the little town, and invitingly, across the bay.

Slim Whitman's 'Rose Marie', echoing round the harbour, as all the happy families took their seats, upon the open top deck. Brothers and sisters, moms and dads, uncles and aunts, granddads and grans, and my mother and us. It must have been heart-rending, but I heard no sighs and saw no tears.

Then Percy James was back and the game was afoot. Out in the early morning, fishing for mackerel, who gave themselves up to us 'towny's', fishing with running lines. Blustery walks right over Sharkham Point, with guillemots jostling for position on the craggy cliffs, and buzzards hovering, wings angled against the wind. Ice-creams on Goodrington's wonderful red sandy beach, with green, brass-chimnied Great Western engines, passing right through the resort, puffing merrily down to Kingswear.

Mussels and whelks on the prom at Teignmouth, writing our names on slips of paper and hiding them in Cockington's old forge thatched roof, watching the packed holiday expresses disgorge their not-yet car drivers, all bursting with anticipation to kiss each other quickly.

Then all too soon, away up the steep climbing road that led us out of Brixham and out of holiday land, leaving the fishing boat klaxons, the steamers hooting, the fish and sea-wood scents, rising from the busy harbour, and carrying all across the waterfront, "My Rose Marie, I love you, I'm always thinking of you .....", fading slowly into the Devon memory.

Dad was one of six brothers and a sister. His father was a farmer and in his day, farm-owners didn't employ hands to work the land, they got married and produced their own.

We used to visit them all, on a rotation basis. I don't think any of the other brothers ever had a car. They were all small-holders, and on our calls, there was always fruit and vegetables to be bought and sampled. Bought, mark you not donated, "there you are Perce, marvellous strawberries, two bob a punnet at Kidder market, you can have 'em for a shilling." Uncle George had one of the first battery-hen sheds in the country, and this gave us the chance to sample fresh eggs, straight from the production line, so to speak. Only two and six a dozen.

Though our visits were regular and the time spent was chatty and interesting, there was always a distance between the brothers, I felt it even then. As I grew up, I respected Dad, but we were never really close, neither of us knew how. There wasn't time. Neath Bros governed every aspect of life and took priority over everything. I vowed to myself that I'd never let that happen in my own life, but it almost did. The work ethic and the awful burden of guilt are impossible to shrug off, and a life ruled by these two imposters is such a deep-seated, personal crisis, it's difficult for others, not themselves afflicted, to understand and come to any sort of terms with.

At home I learnt how to use a scythe and a grasshook. Whilst not the most useful of skills for a thrusting twentieth century teenage go-getter, but the man who hadn't got them, would be talking to you without both feet and six inches nearer to the ground.

I learnt also how horticulture and meteorology are inextricably bound together. Our garden was surrounded by a six-feet high privet hedge, and on days when the rain was driving, hard and vertical, Dad would feel the time was right to hone my scything skills on the soggy evergreen. The hedge was thick of branch and densely leaved, and we both knew the result, before the first upward slash of the blade, but I was always sent out with the same supportive advice, "Don't stay our too long now and don't get wet."

I left school with the summer holidays ahead of me. Dad had asked me what I intended to do, and being a meticulous planner, I told him I had no idea. He told me to take some time off, get away somewhere and think it all over carefully. He never asked me to join the family business, not once.

I went on the High Street Raffle run, spent the next day sitting by the brook with an awful hangover and carefully took stock. The next day I started work for my Dad.

Working as the 'gaffers son', is never an easy situation and I went through the usual 'bedding in' process. That meant a stand-up fight behind one of the vans, with one of the trappy driver's, or mates, every other day for a couple of weeks, until I passed the entry exam and they accepted that I wasn't getting paid more than them, whether I turned up for work or not. You know, the usual, mindless, rubbish.

Finally, after leaving a few highly personal notes regarding some of our staff and a couple of my teeth, in the suggestion box, I settled down and with a succession of decent blokes, enjoyed some good years on the road and in and out of the pubs of England.

I only ever saw my father cry once.

I'd returned home from work to find the house in silence. Dad was alone in our hallway, sobbing gently into his cupped hands. I was too embarrassed to ask why and walking in to our living room, found Uncle Vic, ashy-faced, sitting at the desk. "The old guvnor's dead" he said. Without another word, he got up and went out.

Dad would take me down to the yard, first thing in the morning, then our path's wouldn't cross again, unless he dropped in, on our loading up, to give us a helping hand with special packing or somesuch.

"It's always poor Percy who has to get the bloody job moving", a regular clarion call, as he thundered through each day, driving from job to job in his beloved Humber Super Snipe, giving each crew about thirty minutes of whirlwind activity, to speed them on their way.

Poor Percy was truly ubiquitous.

John Mundy, a pipe-smoking, whiskey drinking philosopher, who doubled as Dad's doctor, had told him on several occasions to slow down. Two small heart 'pulls' had proved his diagnosis correct, but my father was a driven man and thought he was indestructible.

On a misty September morning in 1968, following yet another raucous night out with Bert Nichols in Great Yarmouth, I rang the office to see if there was a return load for us to run back with. It was the usual practice.

Uncle Vic answered the phone, "The old guvnor's dead". He began to heave and sob gently. I put the phone down. The drive to Bromsgrove was the longest journey I've ever endured.

Years later, recovering from my heart attack in Cornwall, my doctor said to me, "Your father gave you many things, narrow arteries was one of them, but he didn't know that."

There was time to reflect, as I recuperated at home, following the fun and games in Cornwall. It was a warm and dry Spring and I spent my days in the garden, with my thoughts and a wonderful male Blackbird. I sat outside every day and he became accustomed to me. As the days progressed, I took him bread and water and he soon came to my hand to feed, and even onto my lap whilst I was preparing his lunch.

When I did my convalescent walks, each one a little longer, as the days passed, he accompanied me, even riding on my shoulder. It was truly remarkable and I came to see him as my talisman, my symbol of renaissance.

He was in prime condition, gloriously plumed in night-velvet black, bright yellow beak and an impossible to fathom depth in his shining eyes. It was a vigorous contrast to the stumbling, faltering, fearful invalid that was by his side, but together we prospered.

I became stronger and more confident, and my walks took me out of the garden, around the quiet streets.

Blackie went about his bird business and eventually set up home, with his new mate, in the honeysuckle bush. I saw him intermittently, as spring turned to summer, then one day he was gone. I think of him often. I have always been a keen bird watcher and I learnt much about him and his species, during those truly halcyon days.

I thought also, how little time I had spent with my father. In our few quiet times together he had always given me sound advice. I didn't take it. At the end of one long, tiring, sweaty day's slog, I'd shouted at him, "They should do away with all old bastards over 50 years old." He said "Think about that again, when you're 49."

So, with his passing, I forged on, bearing the family standard; a furniture remover rampant, in a sea of Anglo-Welsh contradictions.

On my good days, the dry wit and humour of the valleys, but with Llewellyn's capacity for simmering vengeance and depressing self-doubt. An appreciation of music and poetry, choral singing, beer and rugby football, a delight in the females of the species, but doomed to live in a constant romantic fantasy, ever surrounded by half-subjugated jealousies.

What a cocktail of sweet, stinging pain, but what a towering life, these gifts he gave me, and a time to use and enjoy them, longer than his own.

I honour you always, Percy James.

My mother, sister and I, followed him in silence to the crematorium in Worcester. A lengthy cavalcade of Bromsgrove people followed us. My father and I had moved the homes, the possessions of many of them, to start a new life.

Bearing a wreath, a Neath Brothers furniture van brought up the rear of the sad procession.

Percy James and Margaret

CHAPTER FIFTEEN

Ghost Riders in the Guy

Uncle Vic was my father's younger brother. I didn't realise how special he was until I grew up and 'put away childish things'. I can remember him always in our house. The two brothers ploughed on through life together, in sickness and in health, in the ever demanding marriage that conceived the all consuming child; Neath Brothers Removals.

In my early growing up days, I remember still, the side-mouthed sniggering of the drivers, and the alarmed demeanour of my mother, after yet another 'boardroom meeting'. After raised voices, bumps and thumps, they'd both appear, hang-dog faced, Vic with maybe a thick lip and Dad, it always seemed to me, with a darkening, puffy eye. Until they were both too old to fight, company decisions at boardroom level, always went down to the knuckle.

As Lady Eden remarked, "The Suez Canal runs through our drawing room", so Neath Bros vans not only ran through our dining room, but they stopped to fill up with petrol as well.

The 'office' was a roll-top desk in the corner of the room and throughout the day and night, a steady procession of drivers clocked in and out of work. Dad would be handing out delivery notes, expense money and instructions, whilst he and all of us, were eating our evening meal. This could, and often did, continue late into the night, including Saturdays and Sundays. It was not unknown for the final reporting crew to be knocking on the door after the epilogue dot had faded from the TV screen. Frank and forthright debate, or a 'fucking good row', as it really was, between my mother and father, regarding this dreadful intrusion into our family life, was a regular feature of my childhood days. Looking back at this woeful, destructive period in the lives of mom and dad, not to mention my sister and me, perhaps I paint too harsh a picture. It wasn't every night of the week, only about five or six.

It all began at Pensax, where my father, his five brothers and his sister, were born and grew up. The village school was hard by the church, as was the way of it, a hundred and more years ago, and right up to the nineteen fifties, when the education in cerebral and spiritual matters progressed together, intertwined in that particular English way.

The little school is long ago closed, but I have often walked up the winding path to the church, especially in summer, when the walkway becomes a bee-buzzing, honeysuckle scented, blackbird singing bower of tranquillity. Head stones in the yew tree shaded church yard, give evidence of my family forebears, who trekked out of South Wales, leaving the coal-scarred hills of Glamorgan for the rolling greenery of Worcestershire, settled here and made this land theirs for ever, 'Land of my fathers'. The path spirals up to the church, but a steep escarpment also served as a descent for countless dare-devil schoolboys, and it was here that Uncle Vic tumbled to the lower ground, and dealt his head a sharp blow. He was to suffer persistent mental problems throughout his life, all caused by this fall, so the family always believed. It punctuated his genial, happy go lucky life with dark and frightening days, but such was his radiant good humour outside of these, perhaps, as Dryden says,

"There is a pleasure sure

In being mad, which none but madmen know!"

School days and life itself, was so very different then, and standing up on the church hill, I've looked down and found it easy to imagine my father and all the children cavorting and chattering in the little playground below.

My dad always spoke in awed tones of their headmaster, whom they called 'Nimrod', whether this acknowledged his prowess as a hunter (of absentee children one supposes), or merely that he was himself a great enigma, was never made clear. However, the inspiration of awe needs no explanation.

So the brothers grew into their manhood and all were sent out into the wide world with endowments from their father. Three of them set up small-holdings within shouting distance of the church at Pensax, and their children live there still. Eric was the black sheep and joined the army, serving in India. He was a charmer, a natural salesman and cajoled himself into the post of master of horse in a cavalry regiment. Just before the second world war, he endeared himself even further to the family, by marrying a German girl. He was a man who knew how to press all the wrong buttons, at all the right times.

I met him later in life and went out drinking with him on a couple of occasions. He was a revelation in conservation. By now he'd become a brigadier (retired) and could call the birds down out of the trees. He always left the pub company gasping in admiration and invariably lighter in pocket. But he was bloody good value.

As a footnote to Eric, I have to record that he was the only man I ever knew who started a fight, at a funeral wake, in the family-owned pub, with his own brothers. As we all sat black-garbed and sombre, in the little snug at the Bell at Pensax, Eric chose to break the mood with a toast. He stood, cleared his throat, and raising his glass, intoned "Here's to the next." Uncle Vic caught him with an uppercut, Uncle Arthur blacked his eye and the other two brothers jumped on him. The unseemly skirmish was finally halted by my Aunt Hilda, who owned the pub. A plaque marks the spot where he fell. Dad and Uncle Vic, meantime, went out to start their new life together. Despite their boardroom battles, Dad always looked after Vic and they stayed together in business until death did them part. I'm really glad that they did.

My sister and I were brought up in the umbra of planet N.B. and I was totally intoxicated by traveller's tales from the drivers, and couldn't wait to get out on the road with them. From the age of about eight, I was accompanying them at weekends, folding up packing materials, fetching and carrying small items to and from the van, and best of all being allowed to start up the vehicles, and soon, to drive them out of the garage, out into the yard and fill up with diesel. I was doing proper grown-up stuff.

I went out more and more on weekends, and invariably I was teamed up with Vic and his mate. I was soon able to pack the van, wrap and pack glass and chinaware in our wooden tea-chests, and eventually learnt how to dismantle, then re-assemble, a full size concert grand piano.

Oh, how that's come in useful over the years. But this, by any other name, was work and it was the travel that fired my imagination. I was now beginning to accompany Vic on nights' out, a term that he took almost literally, as he could never bring himself to stop driving.

Rolling through some drab, northern industrial town, at God knows what time of night, I'd spot a B and B, or a small hotel, and point it out. "No Bruce lad, we'll just push on to Clitheroe, it'll save more driving in the morning." Save more driving! We'd probably been on the road since about 5am. In those days it could take twelve hours to get up to Glasgow; Germany had its autobahns, we had Warrington swing bridge, on the trunk road to Scotland. This could hold you up in a ten mile traffic jam, for at least a couple of hours, then you'd crawl on through Wigan, Preston, Lancaster, and over Shap fell, at an average speed of about fifteen miles an hour.

Apart from the drawback of being a murderous, war-mongering, cruel megalomaniac, Hitler had seen the future, and it was motorways. He'd had the idea on his day trip to Poland, when he realised that with a fair wind, a decent strip of tarmac, and a Tiger tank, he could drive to Warsaw quicker than we could get up the A6 to bonny Scotland.

We came to camp out at some interesting locations. At the aforementioned Clitheroe, we stayed at the Salvation Army Hostel, on thoughtfully provided, rustily sprung camper beds, the grid patterns of which, I can still define on my back to this day. Then it was six o'clock reveille, a cup of tea and a Mars bar for breakfast, all in, half a crown a night. Then out into the Lancashire dawn, fit and ready for another fifteen hour day.

The annexe of the Ex-Servicemen's Club at Catterick.

It was, of course, late at night when we booked in, I asked the steward if we had running water in our room. He said yes, if it was raining, He wasn't joking. The 'sink' was suspended on a trestle table, half in and half out, of a hole in the bedroom wall. A drought was obviously in force, there was a skimming of liquid in the sink, but it was an unpromising shade of green; and moving. We left without sampling the breakfast. I could see why the servicemen were ex. I also came to recognise fellow guests at the club, when we bumped into them in the transport cafes. They had green faces.

The house of ill repute in Alnwick.

Alnwick is an historic town in Northumberland. Hotspur lived here in the towering castle, before moving south to seek fame and fortune in London, and to found the football club in Tottenham. We arrived here, late even for Vic's standards, and booked into the house, where the darkness was more powerful inside than out. As my eyes grew accustomed to the gloaming, the outline of a huge cauldron, suspended beneath a tripod, became apparent, steaming and bubbling gently. It was the evening meal.

Then, from impossibly opaque corners of the room, the sounds of other guest's already on the dessert course. Ever quickening vowel-sound only expressions, punctuated the misty, broth aroma'd air, then through the shadowlands, dim outlines of stockinged legs, forty five degree raised with white-shoed, twitching feet, marble grey buttocks plunging in and out of the clinging darkness.

"Double double, toil and trouble;

Fire burn and cauldron bubble."

It was Macbeth, with all the witches upstage, having a shag.

The Green Dragon in Horsham was a pleasant eighteenth century inn, full of unpleasant, twentieth century welsh constructions workers. It's one of the truisms of life, that if you enter a pub at 10.30 pm, stone cold sober, your sense of humour is never going to coincide with the boys who started at 5.30 pm. Their jokes weren't funny, Wales as a land of song, in tune, was a concept alien to them, and I've never been able to hit it off with anybody who has piss steam rising from his trousers. We had a pint and went to bed.

We lay staring out through lace-curtained windows, at the mellow Sussex moon. Only a 'Vic night out' could have ensured that we were sharing a large, eight bedded room with the Newport numpties, still steaming and caterwauling in the bar beneath us. Eventually, cursing and belching, Gwent's finest stumbled and spewed, literally, into the room.

They couldn't find the light switch, the blind leading the blind drunk. They couldn't find the wardrobe, clothes torn off and hurled in heaps on the floor. They couldn't find their beds, uproar as they crashed into each other, oaths as they collided with iron bed-frames. They couldn't find the lavatory, nor even the door they'd just come in by. Giving up in expletive despair, they stood, gibbering, naked, and pissed on the floor. The room was filled with urine rainbows. We were in a big top filled with clowns. Silent observers in a piss drenched, multi coloured, vomit scented, foul mouthing, bellowing, sub-human circus.

The next morning we all ate breakfast in painful silence in the bar. The weight of their combined relief the night before had caused the dining room ceiling to collapse. I'll bet the insurance people thought that really was taking the piss.

These were just a few of the interesting times I spent with my Uncle. There were many others, all of them memorable and very, very, different. He had an absolute genius for turning the mundane into the extraordinary.

In my early days with him, we were always together in an old 'Guy Vixen', four cylinder, petrol-engined pantechnicon vehicle. It was like its driver, a unique, rattling old curiosity. They had outstanding steel radiators, the filler caps of which were screw-down heads of Indian chiefs, in full war-bonnet head dress. If Rolls Royce's 'Spirit of Ecstasy' passed a Guy on the road, she went back into the glove compartment and had a fag, to regain her composure.

I have a picture of the Guy, brand new, with my father standing at the driver's door. Even this old photograph can't conceal the pride in his eyes. They've all gone now, the motor, the men, the factory where she was built in Wolverhampton. 'Ghost Riders in the Sky' was a popular song, still playing on the radio, when I began my odyssey with Uncle Vic.

He was a cantankerous, infuriating, warm, funny, caring and unique human being. He was my Dad's brother, and I loved him very much.

I see us still, driving relentlessly down another endless road. The pale moonlight cuts through the darkened cab and throws his profile into sharp relief. Stubbly chin, hair askew, but eyes fixed studiously on the oncoming highway: "Ghost Riders in the Guy".

CHAPTER SIXTEEN

Faith, Hope, No Charity Cup

England had won the Football World Cup at Wembley on that glorious July afternoon in 1966. Or, with the wonderful understatement for which the British people used to be renowned we had, as the Football Association put it, in their official souvenir programme, triumphed in the Final Tie, match number 32. With or without due deference and humility, I don't foresee anyone writing that opening statement ever again, with a different year in it.

I was brought up in schools that played football and my own playing career, tragically curtailed by recurring knee problems, elicited the full gamut of plaudits, from 'average' to 'not bad'. I played with energy, resolve, total commitment, and little discernible artistry or invention. In this respect I pre-dated in my endeavours, all the qualities so widely displayed by England internationals in the twenty first century.

Like Martin Peters, I was years before my time; that's the only way I was anything like Martin Peters.

Realising a long and illustrious career of kicking clever, fast wingers into the touchline crowd, was not to be, I decided to do the decent thing; manage a team.

In the 'Dragoon' pub in Bromsgrove, aided and abetted by several friends and players from Bromsgrove High School, the first unsteady steps towards forming a local league club, slowly became a determined walk to fulfilment.

We formed a committee, (God only knows, why do we do these things?), elected a chairman, secretary, and were extremely fortunate to have a sponsor, who agreed to supply kit, training footballs and goal-nets. We drafted a Byronesque application to the Worcestershire Football Association (Affiliated), and were invited to the pre-season A.G.M. in Worcester. To our surprise and relief, we were accepted into the Worcester Sunday League, Division 5. Back in the 'Dragoon' that evening, after many nights burning the midnight oil, we drank the midnight beer.

Things were moving on apace. Interested local players began to appear in the pub, the usual football horse-trading began. The seduction of players to our colours, usually consisting of getting them pissed, with the promise of a nice new kit, a good cup run, and the chance to play for the best new side in Bromsgrove, was my brief.

Mervyn, who worked for Birds Eye Frozen Foods, secured, in a glorious coup, the use of the company canteen as our home changing room. With stunning logic, as a vote of thanks to the company, we named the club S.P.D. It was thought 'Real Dragoon', or 'A.C. Aston Fields', at this nascent state, was perhaps a little pretentious.

We booked the local playing fields from the Council, decided against putting the sign, 'This is Charford', in the manner of Liverpool, over the changing room door, and sent out official letters to all the players, advising them of the commencement of pre-season training.

I scoured the library for books on soccer training, visited Worcester City's training ground, where their manager Wilf Grant, and team captain Lionel Martin, (ex Aston Villa), were kind enough to let me sit in on their sessions and then was lucky enough to attend, as a visitor, Dave Sexton's Professional coaching evenings at Lilleshall.

From this wealth of material and first hand knowledge of 'real' sessions, I formulated a training manual of a dozen or so different hour-long programmes, designed to tone up the players' fitness and ball skills, and most importantly to generate interest and enthusiasm. Our sessions were always spent with the football during the entire evening. I have never believed in slogging round the field and exhausting everyone with never-ending physical exercises, giving the players their only contact with the ball, in the five a side games at the end; invariably when everyone is too knackered to really express themselves.

New ideas always interested me and I recall Brazil employing a ballet teacher in the early seventies, to develop the concepts of poise, grace and balance, three areas where I considered the Brazilians to be adequately equipped already. I was running Barley Mow F.C. in Worcester at the time, but on reflection, looking at my likely lads, I thought we were more Barley Rambo than Ballet Rambeau. So tu-tu footsy goodbye to that innovation.

Training commenced and I was pleased to find a really good turn-out. Everybody was impressed with the routines, and sensed we were ambitious. There were enough players for a full eleven a side game to conclude each evening, and it was a natural progression to arrange a series of 'friendly's' against local opposition.

As team selection became more focused, and the season's kick off approached, acrimonious outbursts, simmering bitterness, and clandestine back-stabbing began to manifest themselves within our ranks. We knew then we had the basis for a proper league club.

The season began. We were drawn away to Nu-Way Heating of Droitwich for the first match we had ever played in the League. We won 8-0. Surprise and joy were twin emotions at the final whistle. This was fantastic, we had played well; we were going to win this fucking league hands down. S.P.D. had arrived, bring 'em all on.

Three games further into the season, we had only won the first one. Time for what is now called a reality check. The Worcester League was a revelation. In fact some of the teams appeared to have stepped out of the biblical book of the same name.

A succession of 'hard as nails' teams kicked the 'pretty boys' from Bromsgrove into the casualty wards of Worcestershire.

Kempsey, where the 'changing room' was a field that the home team, then spent ninety minutes trying to bury you in. We lost our first meeting with them, by two broken legs to a concussion.

Broadheath, where kick-off was not at 3.00pm, but when the 'Dew Drop' pub closed. Severn Stoke, run by an aristocratic fanatic, Mrs. Leslie Holloway, who swore louder than anyone I'd ever heard, in several languages. Clifton, whose main supporter stalked the touch-line with a twelve-bore rifle, and fired it every time Clifton scored. Not many home defeats there, I seem to remember.

The players, the management, the team, the club, all grew up very fast during that incredible introduction to the 'beautiful game'. We finished a creditable third, but our fund-raising and team 'subs', were not covering the cost of the first aid kits. We were getting through more bandages than ancient Egypt's retail outlet of 'Mummies R Us'.

It had been a roller-coaster ride, much of it in the ambulance, but before we were reduced to a cribbage team, we resigned from the league and joined the North Worcestershire.

Birds Eye Foods didn't appreciate their canteen looking like a ward in the Crimea, and expelled us.

The team had dropped in to Fred Webster's pub a couple of times returning from battle, and Fred had appreciated the way we'd drained his cellar, and maintained our decorum the while. He offered to Sponsor us and gave us his assembly room to change in. We became 'Grasshoppers F.C.'. In an inspired moment, I wrote to the Swiss first division club, based in Zurich, offering to twin with them.

Failing to find us anywhere in the English League structure, they sussed out we were scallywags, but being Swiss, and not wishing to offend anyone, they sent us a pennant, a very nice letter of support, and best of all, a two-foot tall Grasshopper mascot. He sat in our changing room upstairs in the pub, and every match day held pride of place on the bar, when we returned.

Fred kicked off each club night with a two gallon jug of beer, freely donated to the team, if we'd won our match. It was an 'in' pub in those days, and what with raffles and 'Pub Olympics' nights, money began to flow in. Twice, the after dinner speaker, Blaster Bates, he of the demolition and ordnance fame, graciously agreed to come down and entertain us, and the two sell-out evenings raised enough cash for new strips, footballs, nets, first aid supplies, and plenty left over to render player 'subs' a thing of the past. Finally, we secured the best playing surface pitch in Bromsgrove, and the good times indeed began to roll.

None of this would have come to pass without Fred's good nature and hospitality. We will always owe him.

New players wanted to join us, including a couple of ex Rovers boys who really added experience to the team. No need to get the hoped-for signings pissed anymore.

The team was playing some good football, we had the best side in Bromsgrove, forty or fifty people were coming to watch us, home and away. There was a good 'buzz' in and around the club. Fucking amazing.

There was only one cloud on an otherwise perfect horizon. It was Oldswinford F.C. and particularly David Dew, their mentor. They twice denied us the league title and then beat us in the Bromsgrove Charity Cup semi-final on Boxing Day morning. What a Christmas present. Winning that Cup was my burning ambition as a football manager, in front of all the local town players, on the Rover's ground, the Victoria, where I'd stood and watched all those years ago. I had friends on the organising committee and they all willed us to win it, for the town, for the glory, and the almighty lash-up that would surely ensue.

In my fourth and last season in charge of 'Hoppers', we finally made it to the Cup final. It had to be Oldswinford standing in my path yet again, and my last chance to cross swords with David Dew. Two days before the final, a hammer blow. The secretary of the Charity Cup committee rang me to say the Victoria ground was flooded, broken drainage pipes and other problems. We couldn't play the tie. It was transferred to Harris Brush Sports ground, a great set up, a fine ground, but not the one I so desperately wanted. Everybody at the club was disappointed. We had to get our heads up and prepare for the game. The day dawned, about two hundred people had come down to see us. It was very moving. I spoke to David, briefly, before the game, and wished him well.

Seventy five minutes later, I was euphoric. We were beating Oldswinford 6-3. Grasshoppers were going to win the Charity Cup. All the boys had played out of their skins. It was the finest display of football I had ever seen from any team in the league, all our efforts had been worthwhile, the prize was ours.

Then the unthinkable. In the space of fifteen minutes Oldswinford were awarded not one, nor two, but three penalty kicks. To their credit, they had never stopped running, never given up. David Dew had built a gutsy team, but in all honesty I cannot believe to this day, what happened on that field. They scored all three, the referee blew time. No extra time, a replay on Wednesday night.

My players were heart-broken, the crowd drifted away, stunned and unable to communicate their commiserations. David made ten changes to his team for the replay. They were Birmingham and West Mids standard players. We were thrashed 6-1. He had underestimated us in the first match, but did not make the same mistake again.

At least the Victoria ground didn't witness the debacle. I left the club and the team matters in the capable hands of Joe Smith; life at work and at home was difficult, I couldn't keep it all going. There has to be full commitment.

"Where destiny with men for pieces plays:
Hither and thither moves, and mates, and slays,

And one by one, back in the closet lays."

Those marvellous, high octane seasons with the 'Hoppers', compensated for my poor playing career. If I wasn't the greatest football manager, I think I understood the game and the players pretty well, and we managed, between us, to translate the ideas onto the playing field. I always favoured flair players, and while I know that can be seen as a weakness, I'd always rather win 7-6 than 1-0.

With players like Merv 'the Swerve' Thomas, Tony Hall, Frank Bolton and the O'Brien brothers, the team could always provide a bag full of goals and some instinctive tough football.

Defenders were not a lost cause with me and after the chastening season in Worcester, I recruited some boys who would always 'have a look at' somebody for me, if I thought we were all doing too much running for nothing.

My old appetite for wingers never left me and in 'Squarehead', (don't even think it), Gary Sampson and 'Iron legs' Leddington, I had a few clients who shared my taste in biting 'flying machines'.

A final paean of high praise indeed for Brian Raybould, the best player I ever worked with, who could have gone far in the game, but had lots of other things to do. He could be a difficult bastard to deal with, because he was brilliant; that's the way of it, in the round ball game.

"I'll play you until half time Brian, then I'll pull you off."

"Thanks Gaffer, when I was with the Golden Lion, I only used to get an orange."

It's all a long time ago now. Memories jostle each other on the touchline, and I can't help breaking into a smile.

CHAPTER SEVENTEEN

Cold Sweats and Hot Leather

I was a confirmed terrestrial, with no ambitions to add the 'extra' to the description, when at thirty two years of age I made my first aeroplane flight in 1976. This is discounting my earlier parachute jump, and (almost) linear vegetable-rape, in the sprout field.

By then, most of my friends had taken to the skies and discovered the joys of sunshine, sangria and sexually transmitted diseases on the Iberian Peninsula.

Every autumn during daylight hours, anyone under the age of twenty five, catching the 144 bus to Worcester from Bromsgrove, sporting a Mediterranean tan, was keeping an appointment at the 'clap clinic'. How the nursing staff at the old Infirmary must have enjoyed this period of the year. I think it was about this time, that 'spotted dick' disappeared from the hospital canteen pudding menu.

Today of course, most young people have traversed the world by 'plane on their 'gap' year, before they're legally old enough to buy cigarettes. A far cry from my growing-up days, when a gap year meant the one that didn't cost you more than two teeth in the 'Good-night fight' outside 'The Golden Lion', on consecutive Saturday evenings.

The world back then was still a large and mostly unknown place, and in our little town, anyone who knew the way to Birmingham's Elmdon Airport was considered to be a blood relative of Marco Polo, and the only people who holidayed abroad all lived in London.

Looking at passers-by on our streets today, where every other citizen seems to have had a massage with a 'Double Gloucester' cheese, it's truly startling to realise how horribly unhealthy everyone used to appear.

Those shuffling, sighing, staring-eyed, pallid, ill-garbed legions; and that was just the staff at Woolworths. The poor townsfolk, between the months of October and March, resembled nothing so much as the 'Morlocks', the awful, flesh eating subterraneans of H.G. Wells 'Time Machine', who only surfaced under cover of darkness, to carry off the flower-garlanded, lute-twanging 'Eloi'. I think Wells must have stopped for a fish supper at Betty Plants Chip Parlour, one winters evening, and found his inspiration for the novel.

Whilst musing on these matters, I recall Raj, a turbaned Sikh, who used to ply his evening trade in the town pubs, selling "very fine silk, 'Slim Jim' ties, all the way from India, the very best, oh yes." His visits were a highlight of the week. He was very popular; 'quick with a joke and a light of your smoke', radiant of smile, benign of temperament. He lit up the room, and not until he left did the cigarette smog dare to invade the bar again, as he and his suitcase vanished into the night. He was the first person from the sub-continent any of us had ever seen, or met, and he was the only man in town who looked remotely fit and well. I think he came from West Bromwich.

So now here I was, in the quaintly named 'departure lounge' of Speke Airport, Liverpool, feeling decidedly queasy, not helped by the restful décor, apparently applied by a man with a besom broom and a bucket of vomit. I shouldn't be too critical; whoever thought they could entertain an international jet-set, eager to take home warming memories of Britain's fourth largest city, as they took their leisure, and awaited their flights of fancy, in this nightmarish, colour dyslexic, corrugated iron hut, was deserving of the United Nations medal of Universal Optimism.

It's been renamed John Lennon Airport now. I can just hear John saying, "Thanks to all the painters and decorators, who gave up their sleep, their wives and their sense of propriety, to turn this draughty tram shed into a Lancastrian pleasure dome, and I hope you pass the audition....."

We'd motored up from the Midlands, as the elegant travelogue's used to say, my friends Derek, John and Paul, in Derek's dazzlingly white, wondrously new Rover. We were heading for this close encounter with a BEA 'Viscount', only because Geoff Duke's boat had fallen on its side in Heysham harbour. Geoff was a great motor-cyclist of the past and a legend in his own lunchtime, on the Isle of Man. He had entered the cross Irish Sea, ferry charter business with high hopes, but even with his background of death-defying racing on the Island, had decided against attempting to make the crossing of this sometimes violent stretch of water, with 2000 passengers and their accompanying bikes and cars, in a ship listing at approximately 45 degrees. It has to be stating the obvious, but I would not be writing this, had the voyage gone ahead.

Geoff had transferred all his bookings to the airlines, so here we all were; I was exchanging the certain plunge to a watery grave in a lopsided boat, to a green-face frightening, almost certain to happen, plunge to a watery grave, in an antique, overloaded flying machine.

I'd never taken three blokes on in a fist fight, in an Airport lounge before, but I became dangerously near to it, as my three, fast becoming 'ex mates', continued to try to force a full, greasy, English breakfast into my churning stomach.

My mood and spirits rose somewhat, as we filed through the boarding area. Derek was told that on the entry form, under the heading 'Reason for your visit to the Isle of Man', "To get pissed", was not an acceptable answer. He substituted 'A wholesome passion for motorcycle competition and an overwhelming interest in the Island's early Nordic connections, and culture'.

"You berrer gerron then", said the scouse official, "and don't get too pissed and misbehave, or you'll gerra flogging."

We bumped and weaved across the Irish Sea to Douglas, and I sat hypnotised, looking through my wing-seat window, watching the rivets popping and jumping along the cowling around the engine. Thankfully, in what seemed no time at all, the plane was dropping, coming in fast and low, over the cliff-edge that announced our arrival at Ronaldsway Airport I sat, eyes closed tightly, waiting to hit the tarmac: "Can't see much flogging going on", Derek said.

We stayed in Douglas on the first night and Derek's car was shipped over by the Isle of Man Steam Packet Company from Liverpool. It was landed the next morning.

I've always loved the Island. I travelled over many times for the T.T. races, and once or twice for amorous liaisons, one of which became so serious, that I married the liaison; but that, as the novelist's, and the lawcourt's say, is another story.

My old friend the 'Queens Hotel' in Birmingham would have felt comfortably at home in Douglas. There was an air of slightly faded glory about the whole town. From Yates' Wine Lodge to the Villa Marina, everywhere casements were crumbling, floorboards were grumbling, doors were jamming, lights were flickering, paint was peeling and dust was collecting, yawning, and lying back at ease.

Laissez-faire ruled with a rod of velvet. It was wonderfully therapeutic;

the worries of the world left you as fast as sweat in a sauna; even in the late seventies Douglas was still dragging itself, like one of its wonderful horse-drawn trams, into the 1950's.

David Whitfield was singing at the Theatre, Ivy Benson's 'All Girl Band' played every lunchtime in the Villa Marina Gardens. (I always wanted to play with an All-Girl Band, much more fun than a train-set.) 'Grease' was filling the cinema every night, Elton John had his first number one hit, and you could win enough money at the Casino, then the only one in the UK with no limit, to buy Geoff Duke's boat.

We finished our first night in a pub on the sea-front boasting the world's largest grand piano. I fell asleep imagining the world's largest pianist playing "In the wee small hours of the morning."

With the car and a couple of days before the racing started, we had time to 'bash' the Island.

By electric tram to the fantastic wheel of Laxey, over Snaefell, where getting off for an ice-cream, you can see England, Wales, Ireland and Scotland: And as my Dad always used to say, "and they bloody well can't see you."

Horse drawn trams along the seafront at Douglas, by narrow gauge steam train to Castletown and Port Erin, Peel and Ramsey; the lighthouse at Point of Ayre, and with great fortune, a boat across to the Calf of Man, to see the rare Manx Shearwaters.

Then, after trams and trains, and boats and planes, it was time....... the world's greatest motorcycle racing festival, the Isle of Man Tourist Trophy.

I have driven in a car I have to admit, round the T.T. course on 'Mad Sunday'. 'White knuckling', and petrified, my face a concrete concentrated mask, as dry, hard, unforgiving, stone walls skimmed past my windows at convenient decapitating height; at least once every thirty or so seconds, I thought I'd meet my maker. When I checked my course-time at the finish, I found that I'd averaged just over 50mph. Not bad; just marginally 70mph slower than the bike riders.

We met and had a few beers, with some of the competitors after each days endeavours. Great raucous, bellowing, good to be alive, chorus-roaring evenings.

"Remembering you, we will be brave

and strong;
And hail the advent of each dangerous
Day,
And meet the great adventure with a
Song."
Each race day, we left our hotel and moved to a different 'viewing site' around the course. One day on a fast straight (not many of those), then a chicane, then a breathtaking, climbing, twisting section.

Up on the mountain, down at the bottom of Douglas town, on the Ramsey flat; Kate's Cottage, Governor's Bridge; each venue packed with the faithful, all come to see the greatest riders in the world, on the most difficult, dangerous circuit in the world.

Everywhere the full repertoire of skills, were on display. Control at fearsome speed, consummate handling, falcon-eyed judgement, and computer-like timing. Throwing the bikes through an 'ess' at 180mph, only the thickness of the leather between the roadway and the flesh, we watched in awe from behind, beside and above, walls, trees, embankments and ditches, as the methanol gladiators screamed past.

A warm lazy day, we sat with our beers and sandwiches on a low wall, halfway along the Ramsey straight. The sun was high in a clear blue sky, only bird-song and the quiet chatter of the expectant crowd broke the wide rural silence. Then, through a wooded area on the horizon, an insistent, rising drone, that became an angry buzz, as like a swarm of colourful, excited insects, the leading bunch appeared from the depths of the forest. The sound grew in intensity, until the ground and our wall, began to tremble; the leaders streaked, too fast to recognise, past us like wasps shot from catapults, followed by the charging, chasing pack.

With their appearance, we'd all jumped behind the safety of the wall, and as they disappeared, they sucked the vacuum of silence in behind them once again. Visibly shaken and exhilarated, we reclaimed our sitting places, and before we had breath enough to speak, they were all two miles away.

During the celebratory meeting that attended the Island's millennium year, for the final race we were fortunate to have seats in the main Grandstand, on the finish line in Douglas. We had watched a cavalcade of riders, past and present, during the morning, including Agostini, Surtees,

Phil Read, and Geoff Duke, he of falling-over boat fame.

It was time to settle back in our seats for the final 500cc race, which was also, poignantly, to be the last appearance on the Island for the legendary Mike Hailwood, 'Mike the Bike', a hero of mine, and thousands more. The old grandstand was full, we were sitting directly above the pit area, and the rasping, throbbing, engine-tuning continued relentlessly beneath us. A viscous patina of fuel and oil rose through the wooden benches, and the whole timber built edifice shook with the vibrations, and the coming and going of the crowd, as they took their seats.

Cardboard-cupped beers and charcoal burnt sausages passed along the tiered rows, and metallic megaphone announcements danced and echoed through the timber temple to the motorcycle. Hailwood was at the start-line, I had a warm beer and a cremated sausage, I looked to my left and couldn't believe my eyes. John Surtees, the only World Champion on two and four wheels, was sitting beside me.

The flag dropped, and with a roar, the racer's shot from the start-line, down the hill, through outlying Douglas, and then away into the country, not to be seen again for about eighteen minutes; the time it would take these supermen to negotiate 37 of the most difficult and harrowing miles in all road racing. We all chatted animatedly to Surtees, who was generous, knowledgeable and gracious, and signed all our programmes.

Everyone wanted Hailwood to win, but, leading on the last lap, he went 'touring' on Snaefell and Alex George pipped him to the post. I'm sure even Alex felt awful, winning by default, I truly believe he wanted Mike to win as well. What a day, what memories. We floated down to earth on the pit-stop oil cloud, and repaired to the nearest bar, to drink something that was actually cooler than our own body temperature.

A last-night blow out in the hotel in Ramsey, where Derek kindly loaned me the Rover keys, to take the drummer home. We percussionists always stick together, and anyhow, she was a better player than me, was considerably prettier and had much longer legs. I told her she had great rhythm and lovely brush-work; she said thanks for the lift, gave me a good-night kiss and promised to see me next year.

All that remained to be done was to post home the obligatory boxes of Manx kippers, golden yellow, with a taste and texture without equal.

The voyage back was courtesy of the Steam Packet Company. There were only two ways to cross the Irish Sea; either drinking and laughing on a millpond, or four hours in a heaving, thundering, maelstrom, that made the Roaring Forties look like Northfield Swimming Baths.

It was always a give-away if the priest got on the boat in Douglas.

Fortune favoured us on this trip, we all got gently tipsy with the priest (who'd obviously and thankfully) got it wrong this time, and arrived back in Liverpool's Pier Head in reasonably good order, and for once, not the same colour as the kippers.

We clattered down the gang-plank, picked up the car and forged out into the Merseyside traffic.

Time to lie back in the Rover, as Derek piloted us back to Worcester.

Sounds and pictures elbowed each other aside through my mind. Bobbing across in the little boat to the Calf of Man, revving engines, the mingling smell of oil, methanol and sausage, Laxey's slowly turning wheel, the colour of the sea at Port Erin at dusk, laughter and good beer in the pubs and marquees all round the Island, and in the background, everywhere, Elton John and Kiki Dee "You're the one that I want………"

CHAPTER EIGHTEEN

Up the Creek with Crabs

We are on British Caledonian's West African 'stopper', calling at all stations: Dakar, Banjul, Freetown, Monrovia, Abidjan, Accra and Lagos. The B-Cal jet, like a giant gold and blue mosquito, hops on and off the capital faces of the countries that gloried in the harrowing nomenclature of 'The White Man's Grave'. Pauline often noted that my choice of fun destinations left something to be desired. All along this coastline, prison fortresses on harbour islands, bear witness to that most awful trade in people that formed the basis of the world's most dire economy. As the African's were shipped out to the New World, the European imperialists planted their standards, and their sickly countrymen, in the Old World. An economy indeed built on the currency of blood and bones. Africa today cashes its own cheques.

Our destination is Banjul, once known as Bathurst, named after the English Earl who governed here. It is the capital of Gambia, a country completely surrounded by its much larger neighbour, Senegal, and on the map appears to be the mouth of the face of that country, looking out into the wide Atlantic Ocean.

On touchdown, on a landing strip that disappeared into the forest, the plane door opened and we stepped out into an inferno. We also took our first, sweat-soaked steps into a country occupied by its neighbour, and under martial law.

Our tourist agent had absent-mindedly forgotten to mention this detail, but none of the locals seemed at all concerned by the perimeter soldiers, Kalashnikovs at the ready, keeping what the politician's call a 'high profile'.

The customs men were quite willing to chat about it and said there was nothing to worry about, this sort of thing happened two or three times a year, and when they really wanted to make a sabre-rattling point, they'd have a pop at the incoming air-liners. I remember thinking, 'I hope they're in the same laid-back frame of mind when we come to take off; if they let us come back to take off'.

Our luggage appeared and so did a London taxi,, driven by Abraham, who, by the time we arrived at our hotel, had already become our duration guide to West Africa, and was diligently planning the rest of our holiday for us. He told us he knew everything that was going on in the country and everybody that was doing it. It proved to be true and it proved to be extremely useful.

The hotel was about ten miles from Banjul, on the most beautiful, palm-fringed beach. Great sea-eagles beat up and down the water line, skewering into small silver fish as they rolled out of the surf. There was not a building, or a person to be seen, and only the crashing of the tide as it signed its name on the pure white sand, broke the silence of eternal Africa.

Our residence was one of only four in the country, at this time, all planned, erected and owned by Scandinavians. The architect was obviously suffering from home-sickness, and the central hall and all the bedroom apartments, were in the style of fjord-side chalets. Opulence was the watchword here and everywhere, from the understated luxury of the living rooms, to the lavish restaurant and exotically marbled swimming pool, money was talking, and very loudly. On our first ramble through the beautifully manicured gardens, catching sight, occasionally, of the high-pitched chalet roofs, it was not difficult to become aware that here in this foreign field, a corner of it was forever Norway.

Dining here was an unforgettable experience. There was shellfish of every kind, prawns and crayfish as big as man's palm, and lobsters large and strong enough to climb out of their aquarium, and clean its panes of glass from top to bottom with a mop. The fish displayed at every mealtime would have over-stocked several McFisheries stores, and an average sized English allotment would have been denuded each evening to provide the vegetables. The dessert table groaned with fruit of shape, size and colour that we had never seen before. Chablis ran like water and we ran after it. It was truly a gourmand's fantasia, relegating the horn of plenty to a Tesco mini-store. We decided we liked the place.

I awoke the next morning to catch the eye of a bright green gecko, who continued, without undue interest in me, to pad, upside down across the bedroom ceiling, on his huge, flat sticky feet. As I glanced across at Pauline, I was about to ask her why she was balancing red snooker balls on her arms and neck, when the whole room shook violently, and a

'Mirage' fighter jet thundered overhead, so low you could see the pilots low-flying proficiency badge on his shirt pocket. Well, this certainly made a change from "Good morning campers, hi-de-hi".

My quicksilver mind grasped the situation in a trice.

Pauline was about to make a break of at least thirteen, playing upper-body snooker without a cue and war had broken out in the skies above our chalet, between Senegal and Gambia. I fell out of bed, cricked my back, called for the nurse, and ordered Mango and Chablis for breakfast, in that order. The nurse was like Sir Thomas More, "a man for all seasons", but she was a woman. She told me that Pauline was experiencing a particularly violent malaria attack, my back would be ok if I could stop falling to the floor whilst watching upside down tropical lizards, the supersonic alarm clock driver was on his way to Dakar for his coffee and cornflakes, (same time every morning), and yes, she'd join us for Mango and Chablis. Within a couple of hours, the malaria tablets began to batter the snooker balls into submission, and everything in the mosquito tent looked rosy, and blurred.

Mid morning, we strolled through the wonderful gardens to the compound gate, and there as if by magic, appeared Abraham. He said we'd go down to Banjul and do the full capital tour. It was once an important jewel in the Commonwealth crown, and British influence was still apparent. The palladian architecture in the 'diplomatic quarter' echoed its colonial past, and nowhere was the past more poignantly preserved than the cricket pitch, adjacent to the town's most striking building, the official residence. I was amazed to find the area roped off and its privacy respected. Sprinklers were at work on the wicket! It was the only strip of green in all of dusty, hot, Banjul.

We walked at ease through the teeming streets, through throngs of smiling, friendly people. The swirling patterns of the ladies robes, in tie-dye batik, created a wild kaleidoscope of riotous colour. A conga line of customers pursued their purchases, through the haggling, gaggling markets; industrious men sat at small wheels and anvils at the roadside, forging knives, forks and a myriad other metal implements, from base, uncompromising metal. Children joined in our wake, as we snaked our way through Banjul's alleys, the layering smells of fish, fruit, baking bread, spices and cooking meats, assaulting and delighting the senses.

Bicycle bells rang, the few cars horns hooted, barrows and carts darted in all directions, to be swallowed up in the human tide, flowing like watery fingers into a rock pool. Real urban Africa, before the tourist invasion and the corporate hucksters and their 'golden arch' global economy had arrived, to wreak the disempowering havoc of international blandness, here and all over the world.

Suddenly we were out of this benevolent beehive and into the quieter, cooler environs of the harbour. Out along the breakwater, where a small barred-windowed fortress stood as a grim reminder of the earlier trade that was once transacted here.

For countless thousands of West Africa's people, this was to be their last contact with their homeland, the view through those bars their last sight of it, before the long and terrible journey to the Americas.

Abraham and the even younger descendants of those slave people, sat down with us at a roadside café and we all ate 'bushfire', the local, and very apt name for the mouth-burning dish of meat and rice, and tried to extinguish the flames with beer and soft drinks. We must have been at least thirty strong by this time, and when the reckoning came, the whole feast cost about three pounds. We ate no meal, in better company, in all of Africa.

Life developed a routine of sorts. One day on the white sand, where the only conversation was likely to be with the lady melon-sellers, sashaying gracefully along the length of the beach, in their wonderful technicolor robes, the melon's as big as beach balls, perched precariously on their heads. "Melona, Melona", the cry was carried away by the breaking surf. One of these fruits was ample for a day; deftly halved with a glinting machete, the colossal cantaloupe filled ones ears and mouth simultaneously, and served as a coracle, when hours later, it was emptied of its luscious flesh.

Then a day with Abraham, who now brought his friend Christopher, a vital, well spoken, and extremely loquacious, young man about town. He was about fifteen, going on forty five. His ambition, he told us, was to get to Dakar and eventually to Paris, where he would open a fabulous restaurant. He enthused about food and cooking to an extraordinary degree, for a boy of such tender years. I'm willing to bet 'Maison Christopher' is pulling in the high-cuisine aficionados of the French capital, at this very moment.

I have to say, that usually I like to do my exploring on my own terms and not in any organised party, but the 'Abe and Chris Roadshow' was a very different way to see the real Gambia. We took a boat down the Gambia river, deep in the interior of the country, where we indulged our passion for bird spotting. The country has more indigenous species than any other on the continent, and we 'ticked off' over a hundred and twenty, in a surreal silent trip of several miles, the forest vegetation coming right down to the water edge and not a soul to be seen or heard. Only the calls and cries of the avian chorus, as they swooped and soared above and around us, our vision always full of brilliant, flashing colours. An aquatic, psychedelic experience.

Another trip to the last remaining area of bushland, where careful walking was high priority, with termites and soldier ants, marching to unknown battlefields, colourful snakes snoozing in sunny corners, web-hanging spiders like plate-sized ink blots, and gyrating dragonflies as big as Chinook helicopters. Shy mongoose families snuffled and shuffled into the safety of their burrows, whilst high above us a bawling, screaming, regiment of unseen monkeys, crashed through the forest canopy, to disappear into a silence broken only by the high pitched, intermittent drone of the cicadas.

Thrilling and exciting though this wonderful safari was, I was beginning to wonder if we would ever get out of the forest, when we suddenly arrived at a clearing, complete with thatch-roofed 'restaurant', more smiling children, and amazingly, Abe and Christopher. We all sat and tucked into more 'bushfire', and its Coke or Fanta antidote. It seemed that each meal got hotter, but we were determined to meet the challenge.

The entire clearing was alive with humming birds, they came to our tables and droned just inches from our faces, their wings a blur of impossible speed. As the sun began to dip sharply in the sky, as it does in Africa, we gathered ourselves and prepared to leave. It was only now that we noticed, in a corner of the clearing, a cage, about twelve feet square, and in it, a mangy, dejected looking lion. Abraham told us he was the only lion in Gambia. How sad it was to see the king of beasts, the only prisoner in his own realm.

On another day whilst Pauline spent the day beside the pool,

Christopher and I went to the football stadium to watch the Banjul Lions play the Indomitables of Georgetown; no Rovers or Wanderers here. We sat high in the terrace of the old concrete structure, in shorts and open necked shirts, brilliant sunshine reaching every corner of the ground. A new band of followers surrounded us and I gave out some Aston Villa programmes I'd brought with me. I bought newspaper cones full of popcorn and ground nuts, and a whole box full of tins of Fanta. We settled down to watch the game. There were about five or six thousand people happily shouting, laughing, cheering and continually blowing whistles, throughout the entire ninety minutes.

Mine was the only white face in the stadium.

Banjul won 2-1. All the players enjoyed themselves immensely, and virtuosity was on display, from backs and forwards alike. Teamwork was perhaps not too high on the agenda, but the individual skill-shows were hugely appreciated by the good humoured crowd.

There is a bravura in African football, seen only elsewhere, in the wonderful play of the Brazilians. They have embraced the close, fast passing game, whilst continuing to allow their players to fully express themselves individually, and have become almost unassailable at footballs highest level. Our own Stanley Matthews spent much time on this Continent in the sixties and seventies, and was so impressed with them, that he was sure they would win the World Cup by the year 2000, with one of their nations' teams. Since then, however, their coaching has been taken over by hard-headed Europeans, whose mantra is 'work-rate'. Military drilled, robotic, defensive 'pattern' play, where flair is subordinated to the common cause of team ethic. That golden vision of a World Cup win looks further away now than forty years ago.

With the end of our holiday approaching, Abraham surprised us with an invitation to join him and his wife for dinner, following what he called one final 'unusual' safari during the day.

After an early breakfast, we jumped into the trusty taxi and chugged away for about fifty miles, following the river, where it formed the national border with Senegal. We stopped, and whilst Abraham clambered down the river bank, we had time to take in the surroundings. The river at this point was perhaps four hundred yards wide, and the tree-line ran right to the river bank, reminiscent of the Dart, upstream from Dartmouth.

A pair of herons staggered clumsily into the sky, their slow wing-beats the only sounds, together with the gurgling of the slow moving water. Abraham meantime, had pulled a small dinghy from a hidden inlet, and dragged it onto a shoal at the foot of the bank. He gestured to us to keep quiet, and then lobbed a largish stone into the middle of the river. Like figures appearing from a swiss clock, uniformed soldiers stepped forward, out of the trees and scrub on the other bank, at intervals of about thirty yards, to left and right of us, as far as we could see. They were all armed with rifles, and all were pointed across the river and at us. We were paralysed with fear. I closed my eyes and waited for the shots and the bullets to strike me. My mouth was a dry as a Hessian sack, and adrenalin must have been pouring out of my ears. I opened my eyes in time to see Abraham wave his arms at the men, who waved back, then incredibly, melted back into the opposite forest.

"I don't think this is the right day to cross into Senegal" he said, "we'll go to my cousin's compound and have some tea."

It was a short drive to the house, a sprawling, ex-colonial pile hard on the waters edge. Indeed the front garden area was coarse shingle, supporting reed-like plants and interspersed with couch-grass tufts.

The family came out and greeted us enthusiastically, bringing tea and oat cakes, then they all retired indoors, whilst we sat lazily back and tried to bring our blood pressure down after the scary moments earlier in the day.

We must both have fallen into a light sleep, in this calmest of places, with giggling water spouts and a warm breeze blowing gently across the river to soothe, and numb, the senses. As is the way in these instances, I suddenly jolted into wakefulness and opening my eyes, thought I'd stepped into a nightmare. We were surrounded by huge fiddler crabs. I looked around, both I and Pauline were encircled by them, hundreds, some within a foot or so of our chairs. I brought up my knees and, putting both feet firmly on the ground, I admit, preparing for flight, before my unbelieving eyes, as if by magic, they all disappeared. I woke Pauline and hushed her to be quiet; within a few seconds, they appeared again, popping up out of their camouflaged burrows to stare at the intruders. I tapped my foot on the sand and the multitude of heavy-clawed crustaceans crash-dived once again. We spent half an hour playing hide and seek with the shy fiddlers, marvelling at their hearing, with merely the tiniest sudden pressure on the sand, rendering them invisible.

Abraham's family all laughed when we told them about our encounter. When I inspected the sand as we left, there was not a grain out of place, to give away their whereabouts.

For our last evening, we decided to put on the glad-rags for Abraham's generous offer to wine and dine us. I'm so glad that we did.

He duly arrived to pick us up, spot on time, as ever.

We walked out of the compound gate to meet him, and were stopped in our tracks, as he came into view. He was dressed in an ankle length white robe, with black and gold sashes around his waist, and diagonally across his right shoulder. A square, topper-like hat in black and gold completed his regal costume. We were both too overcome to make small talk as the cab took us through the town, and not, as we thought, to a restaurant, but to his home.

It was early evening, but the sun was about to perform its disappearing trick. In Africa day becomes night with small ceremony, and the light was fast fading.

We stepped from the taxi and with magical-timing, Abraham's wife appeared in the doorway, as the gloaming engulfed us. The failing light could not hide her magnificence. She was almost six feet fall, with jet black coiffed hair, and her high cheek-boned face held all the mystery of the Continent. Her floor length pure white robe was augmented by a gold necklace, and gold bangles lay upon her wrists.

I remember telling Pauline later, that I thought she looked 'OK'.

The table was set, in the centre of the room and candles flickered and threw shadows across the walls and ceiling. There were carafes of iced water on hand, as tonight, Abraham had told us, we would taste real 'bushfire'. This we duly did, and all it really lacked, in my opinion, was a fire certificate.

Bathsheba spoke perfect French, and had been to University in Dakar. She told us that despite the current local difficulty, the two countries usually managed to rub along quite amiably.

As we talked, and my eyes became better accustomed to the half-light, I was sure I made out shadowy figures in the corner of the room. Noticing this, Abraham called out to his two teenage sons, explaining that they were not allowed to put themselves forward when guests were present. I asked them to sit with us and they joined in the conversation, and the demolition of the 'bushfire' with gusto. I was particularly pleased with this development, fearing that any more of this flammable dish would render me a victim of combustion.

It was a memorable night on which to end a memorable holiday. I'm convinced that Abraham was no ordinary 'cabby' and would have loved to ask him, but perhaps it was as well not to do so. They were warm and dignified people, in a country of charm, grace, and genuine friendliness.

I feel privileged to have spent even so short a time in their company and in their country. In the ensuing years, in all our travels, Gambia retains a special place in my memory.

Next morning Senegal's troops were playing football outside the airport departure hall, their rifles stacked casually in a heap against the fence. They smiled and wished us all bon voyage.

The BCal giant mosquito revved up, tore down the runway, cleared the monkey filled forest canopy, and powered us back to the real world.

Holiday crowds on Gambia beach

CHAPTER NINETEEN

Margaret Rose

We sat in 'The Talbot', Little London, Worcester. Margaret Wilmott, her daughters Margaret and Dorothy, and tucked away, hidden in the corner behind the table, me. Wilmott was the gang leader, she and her girls were out for a few drinks. It was after ten o'clock, the decibel level was rising, the conversation was dipping below the waist-line.

Other patrons in the full, smokey bar, were dropping their heads, not wanting to make eye-contact with the trio, and shuffling their feet uneasily. The barman was visibly alarmed, and dried the pint-pot for the third time.

It was time for 'Silver Wings'; No, it wasn't a super-hero who appeared when you shouted 'Shazam', or whatever, but the name of Worcester's only Taxi company, and the game was about to begin.

Margaret Wilmott was seventy years old. She was five feet tall and about six feet in circumference. She carried a black umbrella with a ducks-head handle, a black handbag almost half as tall as she was, and wore a flat, black hat in the fashion set by the Giles cartoon gran. She also wore black as her complete ensemble colour; dress, stockings, shoes. It could fairly be argued, that black was her favourite. In this respect she resembled our dear, late, Queen Victoria.

However, as she regularly consumed ten pints of stout each day, had a wider repertoire of oaths and curses than a dockyard matey, often relieved herself by hiking up her skirt in the pub car-park, and could beat any of the Talbot customers in a fist fight, that was where the resemblance ended. She was also my Gran.

Dorothy was known by all as Dolly. I would never have wanted to say 'hello' to her. She was down on a flying visit from Erdington, in Birmingham, a trip I was convinced she made on a broomstick. Now she lived in 'Brum', she was a city girl, so she dressed like a tart. She was daubed in startling make-up, with such an abundance of scarlet, especially her lipstick, she looked like a cheetah who'd savaged a gazelle. If this narrative is giving out the strong impression that I disliked her, then it's doing its job to a tee. I didn't normally take an instant dislike to anyone, but in her case, it saved valuable time. I was proved right in my assessment, when later in life, she was to cause much pain between my mother and me.

The other, and younger Margaret, was my Mom, who was led, hypnotically, by Dolly. It was to be a catastrophic path she trod, because of her older sister, after Dad's death.

However, there were no problems this night, except trying to get the taxi home, when all three, and especially Wilmott senior, were semi-riotously drunk. Gran was banned 'sine die' by the Company, after earlier indiscretions, so a strategy was embarked upon, along the following lines: Some innocent fellow drinker, who didn't know her, (not too many of those left in Worcester), hence the 'head-down' scenario, would be enjoined to phone the taxi under his own name, never, of course, mentioning the lady in black. This done, Gran would slip out of the bar and hide in the car park, this of course was where her colour-coordinated costume paid handsome dividends.

The driver would come into the bar, and Mom, Dolly and I would accompany him to the waiting car, to find, o sweet surprise, Gran already ensconced in the back seat. After an exchange of pleasantries, then expletives, with the incentive of the ducks-head gamp pressing against his windpipe, the driver was usually convinced to take us all home.

On occasions the whole circus pitched up outside Deansway Police Station, then the taxi driver would get a bollocking, and 'Worcester's finest' would have to bring us back. They wouldn't dare try to lock Gran up for the night, they hadn't got enough staff.

I was present on a couple of these occasions, but they were soon to end, as Gran's heroic strength finally ebbed from her, leaving her stranded in her little house in Mayfield Avenue; a shrinking, failing old lady. I'm glad to have known her when she was a lion. Indomitable, raging, battering all before her. What must she have been like when she was young?

My mother was absolutely nothing like her, but later on she showed, she had inherited Gran's inner steel. She was born and grew up in the Blockhouse area of Worcester, a rough, poor, slum area of the city. Her birth certificate describes her as 'machinist in tin factory', but I never did find out where it was.

The whole area was demolished and new small industrial units now flourish, where once a large population struggled to exist, without electricity, gas, and sometimes, even water. I have a wonderful, fading picture of her, taken when she was sixteen years old, in 1932. She was the city's Carnival Queen, and wears her hair tied back in a bun, and has on a white, scoop neck dress, with a red rose at her breast. Over the years the picture has mellowed and fallen back into a soft blue background, giving it an ethereal quality.

How Margaret met Percy I have no idea, but he must have been something of a 'catch', business owner and all, to a machine girl. God knows, looking even now, at the picture, she must have dazzled him.

They were married when Margaret was twenty four and moved up to 196 Worcester Road, Bromsgrove, where they lived until death did them part. Her first child, my sister Gloria, was stillborn. She never told me about her until I was twenty one, when she gave me a cygnet ring for my coming of age.

From the very beginning, as the whole family huddled under the stairway, in the pantry, whilst Hitler's late shift of bombers droned overhead, with their final going-away gifts for the Austin Motors Works, life was never going to be easy for my mother. The glittering prize of marriage to the self-assured man of means, must swiftly have turned into a tarnished trinket.

From the outset, my father and Uncle Vic were the only drivers, and as the war ended, all manner of vehicles were seconded into government usage. I know from later talks with her, that they were sometimes away for days, even weeks, moving equipment around for the Ministry of Defence. The work paid well and the business flourished, more vehicles were acquired, more drivers, the day and night-time relentless migration of people through the domestic home had begun. It was the beginning of a thirty year sentence, imprisoned in a transport office, with no time off for good behaviour.

I'm sure, in the excitement, especially at the start, that neither of them thought of it like that, but the monster eventually consumed us all, and by the time I realised that my home-life had never really existed, I was about to get married myself, and leave it all.

My sister left the bedlam before me, throwing a series of almighty fits, and finally walking out, to live with her partner. We all thought it was really bad form, and despised her for it. But she was closer to my mother and felt more for her, and eventually could tolerate it no more. I know now that she was right, and thankfully was able to tell her so.

Mother battled on, keeping her anguish to herself.

As the nineteen fifties ticked on, and we were all never having it so good, my Dad began to lose the fight to keep the twentieth century at bay. The fridge was probably the first piece of equipment mother had ever been presented with, that had more than three moving parts. This threw the pantry into redundancy. Well almost; cheeses, all fresh fruit and veg, and most meats, never tasted so good, as when they were wrapped in muslin, in front of the airbrick.

The mangle was consigned to the back yard as a piece of retro domestic sculpture, and was soon followed by the dolly-tub and the tin bath. We had a bath and an upstairs toilet fitted, now there's posh, isn't it?

Out went the six inch screen TV, that you could only see with the Hubble telescope, I could pick up the portable radio without a block and tackle, and I played my records on a new 'Dansette', never again having to wind up the old gramophone, which was like starting a P6 Perkins diesel engine, and goodbye to the biscuit tin full of needles.

The whole house was full of whirring, shaking, banging, bumping machinery, doing washing, drying, freezing, peeling, slicing and Lord knows what else. It was like something out of Wallace and Gromitt.

Father had cunningly turned the outside loo into an en-suite, by building a doorway across the outside access to our kitchen, so we could now go to the toilet in the winter time, without waiting in a queue with the penguins. Oh, and for novelty value, a gas heater now meant that the water came out of the downstairs tap in more than one piece.

Time moved on; it was another Christmas Eve, Dad was long gone, mother and I were sitting together in our 'front room' at 196. I had always loved the room, right back to my childhood, when I would bring my presents down on Christmas morning and unwrap them on the floor, in front of the crackling log fire that burnt in the open grate.

The ingle surround was a wonder, with a five-foot high ornate top shelf, with fluted supports, all of sumptuous furnished redwood, and a back plate surround of rich brightly coloured floral tiles, in the Portuguese style. The black-leaded grate, with its logs oozing bubbling, popping resin as they burnt, and the scent of new timber reaching out through the yellow flames, filled the room with warmth and well-being. Floor length burgundy curtains, drawn across the bay window area, completed the snug and cosy ambience of the room.

I poured a drink for each of us, scotch and water for me, and a Dubonnet for mother, and we sat in the comfortable arm chairs, facing each other across the flickering, crackling firelight, as the days light lowered and the dark crept in. After a few moments, without prompting, she began to talk of her days in service at Canford Cliffs near Bournemouth, of the job in the tin works, the Carnival, her family in Worcester (she was one of seven children), courting days with Dad, early married life. She'd never spoken to me about these things before, these amazing, evocative tales of a whole different world. I had no idea.

A whole lifetime was passing between us, as our faces danced in the firelight. How long we sat together, I have no idea; I was light-headed, I could barely see her now through the shadows, as the fire-light ebbed. I rose to leave and walked across to kiss her. She'd told me her whole life story. I'd been her son for forty years and never known any of it. That night I knew my mother for the very first time and felt privileged to have been in her company, and proud to be her son.

Dennis Bosley and my mother had become great friends and got along famously, though sometimes fractiously. He was a good man, a widower, who came to care a great deal for her and spared no expense, nor time, to make her life a better, happier one. She in turn, chided him, bullied him, in a half-hearted fashion, and generally got her own back on a lifetime of loneliness.

They went out together, on holidays and trips, and gently painted the town reddish. They were an item, and despite her pleas to the contrary, they were very good for each other. I liked Dennis very much, I often took a pint with him and we played the occasional game of snooker in the Bromsgrove Labour Club.

I'm eternally glad that they found each other before mother became ill. The illness, when it did come, was short and brutal. She spent her final days in great pain, in the wonderful care of the Women's Hospital in Birmingham.

I picked up Dennis every day and drove up to see her. On what turned out to be her last day, we had just got back after our visit, when the hospital phoned us; it was most urgent. We tore back to Birmingham, but she had already gone. I hadn't been able to contact my sister, I'd lost touch with her, I was distraught. We walked into the ward and my sister, Marina, was there. It was miraculous.

We all held each other in silent, sobbing grief. I looked down at mother, the pain and horror had gone from her face. I kissed her for the last time. She was beautiful once more. She was laid out in a white scoop-neck dress, with a red rose at her breast.

"Age cannot wither her, nor custom stale
Her infinite variety."

Margaret Rose

CHAPTER TWENTY

The Quality of Mercy

Rat on the road. Have 'Sierra' will travel; about 50,000 miles a year for about fourteen years, in fact, I used to say 'I'll be glad when I've had enough', and when it actually happened, it was nearly the last thing I did say.

Like Jesus in Handel's Messiah, though not like him in any other way, we were 'despised'; patronised and impugned, used and abused. I obviously didn't take the job for the status, but, like so many other jobs, because I found myself being shunted out of work. That's why I only did it as a temporary measure, so it's clear that Littlewoods Pools didn't come up with the goods, nor any rich soul who loved me dearly, shuffled off their mortal coil, and left me a bundle of dosh.

My 'beat' was South and West Wales and the entire West Country, so for all those years, the first week in March found me in the Duchy of Cornwall.

After about ten years, they took me to their hearts. Well, not quite, but at least they stopped overcharging me in the pubs, and calling me an emmet. That's Cornish slang for a tourist, (it actually means an ant), but you get the picture. I used to take a whole week to 'do' the county, and as I was away from my creature comforts, and indeed, my creature, I used to pitch up wherever I chose, and by and large, I stayed at almost every seaside town and village on the peninsula.

I was a regular, almost one of Johnny Cornwall's boys. I knew the 'Cadgwith Anthem' and 'Trelawny', the dirty version of the 'Helston Flower Song', and got on pretty well with a jolly barmaid at the Admiral Benbow in Penzance.

I once booked, on the off chance, a night out at a little guest house in Penzance and turned up late at night, to be met at the door by Jean Shrimpton. I was served breakfast by the 'Shrimp'. I'd dreamt of it, but that was only part of the dream; of course it was the only part that came true.

Most nights out weren't so erotically charged, but I did manage to stay at some lovely hotels and Inns, in some wonderful Cornish beauty spots, but as the hotel tariffs and my expense allowance were diametrically opposed, I often had to subsidise the evening from my own pocket.

What the hell; in the course of all those years, I got to know and love the county, and traversed it during all the seasons. I dined and wined in fine country houses, walked out at dawn, on empty golden beaches on March mornings, visited the wondrous secret gardens at Heligan, Caerhays and Trewithen in springtime, and at summers end, and watched the green Atlantic making rough but ardent love to the village harbours in Porthleven and Coverack in robust, stirring winter.

So March of 1989 found me once again bucketing down the A390 to Lostwithiel, I had a builders merchant call to make, but first I stopped for lunch, just outside the town itself in a quiet lane that overlooked the River Fowey. I ate my Cornish pasty, bought earlier in the day at Callington, drank a half-warm tin of Coke and sat out on the grass, smoking my fifth or sixth, cigarette of the day. With bird song and the Fowey chuckling over the river bed pebbles the only sounds, and a light, warm breeze blowing under a clear blue sky, the day was going well.

I had just two more calls to make, I'd already picked up a couple of decent orders and I was booked into the Penventon in Redruth. It was one of my favourite stops in Cornwall. It was a class joint, with luxurious bed chambers, an art deco restaurant with a highly imaginative menu, and works of art, paintings and sculptures in every available free space in the building. There was also a baby grand piano in the dining room. I wondered if the music room had an Aga as it's centre-piece. It didn't.

It was while I was letting my imagination get the better of me, regarding the forthcoming evening, that I began to feel distinctly uneasy. A cold sweat had broken out on my brow and my hair at the back of my neck was tingling, and could I feel a dull ache in the middle of my back? Get a grip, press on, and get parked up.

I completed my calls and rolled into the hotel car park at about half past five. I completed the booking-in formalities, stowed my gear, showered, dressed, and went down for a couple of drinks before ordering dinner. I'd just decided to order the guinea-fowl, when all the lunch-time symptoms returned, this time accompanied by a tight feeling across my chest. I felt sick and went upstairs to my room. I lit up a cigarette; the tightness got worse, I threw up in the toilet basin. I lay down, stood up, walked around, lay down again. The pain wouldn't go, it was getting worse. I knew what was happening, fuck it! I was having a heart attack, in Cornwall; I couldn't be further away from home.

No mobile phones, but a room service telephone. God, it didn't work. I walked down to reception and as casually as possible, asked for the doctor on call's number. I said I felt a bit 'peaky'. What does that mean? The doc was out on his rounds, so I left my room number and name, and went back to my room. I felt distinctly under the weather, but I decided to drive into Redruth and find the local cottage hospital.

This was not so easy, it was now dark and the rain had begun to come down hard. I was not giving my driving my full attention, and becoming desperate, looking for the 'H' sign to save my life. At last I saw it, and pulled up outside the building. It was not a friendly sight. My impression was of a back door to a run-down, two storey budget size castle. No notices or signs that I could see, but a dimly lit bell-push. I pushed, it rang, nothing happened. I was cold and getting soaked, and about to die in a back street of a dreary Cornish mining town. I'd missed my guinea fowl, hadn't had a drink for over two hours, and felt like a bag of shit. What sort of night out was this. I'd had better.

I rang again, cursing, and kept my finger on the buzzer. Suddenly a panel in the door, the size of a letter-box, slid open. In the darkness I hadn't noticed it. I peered through the slit, I was looking into the face of a nun. "What do you want?" "Please let me in, I'm having a heart attack." "You can't come in here." "Why not, for God's sake?" "This is a women's hospital, and don't take the Lord's name in vain." "Well, let me in, and phone for a doctor." "You're not a woman, you can't come in." "You can't turn me away, you're a nun." "And you're not a woman, fuck off!"

The panel slid shut, the rain came pelting down. I decided to drive back to the hotel and die in comfort.

I arrived back at the Penventon, parked up and strode through reception. The girl on the desk looked aghast. When I got to my room and looked in the mirror, and understood why. I was dripping wet through, my hair was lank and lying over my face, which was as white as Father Christmas's beard, and my lips were turning blue.

I lit up another cigarette, and contemplated death, the universe and all that.

My door bell rang, I opened it for the doctor. I saw that 'girl on the desk' look again. He looked at me, sat me down, gave me a shot of morphine and told me what I already knew. Then he phoned for the ambulance, and helped me light another cigarette. I'd just had my first drag, when the ambulance boys arrived for me. They said they'd carry me, I said I'd walk, it'll be OK. I couldn't move.

As they slid me into the ambulance, I saw the full Cornish moon looking down on me. It had stopped raining, and the sky was perfectly clear. Too fucking late, I thought.

CHAPTER TWENTY ONE

Big Little Richard

It was the Spring of 1989 when I met Richard, in the critical ward at Treliske Hospital in Truro, Cornwall.

This place was set aside for patients whose chances of survival were less than 50/50. I was unaware of this when I was on the ward, as indeed were all of my fellow patients. My nurse told me these interesting details, after I'd been moved to a regular recovery area. Of course if you didn't beat the odds, nobody needed to tell you.

In actual fact, I really didn't meet Richard at all, but he was just an arm's reach away from me, for seven days, until he died. He was a small man, a son of Kernow, Truro born and bred, a Cornish man. His loving family came every night to see him and always brought a string bag full of Cornish pasties. There were lots of them, and I could hear them approaching, long before they arrived, down the echoing passageways to the wards. Then, bursting through the swing doors, laughing, chattering, tripping over each other's news, greetings and kisses for Richard, joyful, heartfelt feelings in a wonderful Cornish burr. Then chairs were dragged across the ward, to encircle the bed, pasties distributed, pies steaming in their newspaper parcels, knives, forks, salt and pepper, sauce; the place had turned into the family dining room. I expected dancing, it was like Mr. Fezziwig's Christmas party.

Richard was 'nil by mouth', but now alert, alive, and tucking into his pasty with gusto, as the cheery voices passed their messages round and round his bed, crumbs spluttering, mouths wiped, noses blown; the family business brought up to date.

At last it was time to go, lining up for goodbye's and kisses, "see you soon, Rich", "take care", "be good", "back tomorrow." The happy little procession retraced their steps down the long arcades, their animated voices fading at last to silence.

Then, with the visitors gone, the lights dimmed, the night began. Each night I was in this room, every night was the longest of my life.

There were perhaps ten of us in the ward, a completely open area, with no curtains or barriers between or around the beds. Next to me lay a distinguished looking man, who had a healthy appearance in daylight scrutiny, and who lay and breathed deeply and evenly throughout the many visits of his nurse. But as the light gave way to darkness, he began to whimper and yelp, like a puppy dog. He was attended constantly through the whole, seemingly endless night; I was too shocked to stay awake, but too frightened to fall asleep.

On, I think, the third night, whilst awake between the fitful bouts of sleep, I looked across to him, and through the half-light, I saw the nurse accompanied by a priest. I strained to hear the muted conversation, as he knelt at the bedside, but to no avail, and at last I drifted off again to slumbering nightmares. I woke again before the dawn, staring through the gloom; the light began to stroke the windows, and the priest was gone. My companion's bed was empty.

No one had ever died so close to me before. Whilst I was on the ward, he was the first of four comrades to disappear before the morning's light. I bit my tongue until it bled, to try to stay awake, I have never, before or since, been so terrified of sleeping.

Each night, soon after Richard's wondrous kinfolk had departed, I became aware that he was calling out, quietly, gently, impossible to hear.

One bloodshot Cornish morning, he too was gone. His nurse, a real angel, who tended him with so much more than professional love, told me, when I asked her, what it was that he was saying. She said it was the same thing every night, over and over; "Don't hurt I, please don't hurt I no more." His pain must have been beyond endurance, but he never flinched, nor ever said a word of it, to his marvellous family. I still feel great sadness, tinged with pride that I knew him, in whatever small way.

Little Cornish Richard, such a big, big man.

Sleep quietly now in Truro.

CHAPTER TWENTY TWO

Bruce Lee, Kung Fu and Tea for Two

"O for a muse of fire, that would ascend
The brightest heaven of invention."
There was a period in the late eighties and early nineties, when people used to approach me in pubs, and ask me what the capital of Dahomey was; or the average rainfall in the Amazon Basin, or the highest mountain in the Hindu Kush range.

If you don't know the answers to the questions, don't worry too much. Don't ponder on them, or rush home to your reference books and look them up. Lets face it, you probably don't give a porcupines penis and why should you? But for me, back then, it was different. I wasn't taking the Greenpeace entrance exam, working on my Open University Geography Degree, or planning to walk round the world for charity, with only my childhood teddy-bear for company. No, it was much more serious than that; I was the Captain of the Vine Quiz team, and Geography was my specialist subject.

In pubs and clubs all over the town, fellow quiz-nuts were being subjected to similar grillings. The Quiz League had taken off big-style in Worcester, with four divisions, all playing their fixtures on Sunday evenings. From the offset, it was obvious that it was going to be competitive, and set the pattern for future evaluation of a particular pub's clientele. No longer were houses judged to be frequented by good sports, hard drinkers, dart freaks, or pretty rough characters, but now, either by clever bastards or dumb fuckers. We welded together a team determined to be the former. To see us, in the corner of the lounge, testing each other on our chosen subjects, night after night, the other regulars were certain we were definitely the latter. But it had to be done. We were determined to excel at all costs. Like Bill Shankly said of football, "this wasn't a matter of life or death, it was much more important than that."

It had all started in the "Halfway House" on Cheltenham's Gold Cup day. The landlord, Paddy McGuire, who always used to say, "How fortunate indeed I am, to be born Irish, or my name would have been a constant embarrassment to me." He was the typical Irishman, who lived his life in a three-way love affair with the English language, drink and horse-racing.

Six or seven of us were tucking into a breakfast of bacon, eggs, champagne and guinness, waiting for the minibus to take us to the race-meeting. There was plenty of time for general banter and to select our winners from the Sporting Life; it was seven o'clock in the morning. Paddy had been embroidering the events of the last evening's shindig in the pub, and how a smarty-pants, smug crowd had walked in, challenged the locals to a quiz, and proceeded to beat them hollow. He'd found out they were from the "Sebright Arms" and were the current champions of the local pub league. Paddy was determined to gain revenge and restore the pub's honour. We agreed to form a team and enter the next season, and fired by the Franco-Irish breakfast fare, we vowed to give the 'Sebright' boys the thrashing they so thoroughly deserved.

It was the last thing I remember vowing that day. The hospitality continued in a mobile manner, on our way down to Cheltenham, in much the same mode as in the public bar, but without the solids.

We pitched up at about ten o'clock in a friendly, little hotel that an observer would have thought was in the centre of Dublin. It was full of chatter, smoke and Irishmen, who not only knew, on a personal basis, all the trainers, owners and riders, but had been raised and brought up in the same stalls as the horses.

Someone mentioned that my eyes already looked awfully bloodshot, I remember thinking, he should see them from my side.

We moved on, a platoon in Paddy's army, to the hospitality tent on Cheltenham's fantastic race-course. The Guinness attack on the liver was relentless, and we ventured out into the natural light of day, only to watch the climax of each race, the steaming steeds slamming up Cheltenham's hill to the winning post, their hoof-beats resonating through our plastic Guinness glasses.

Security on the course was very tight, and so were the refugee population of the Emerald Isle. To almost paraphrase Lyndon Johnson, it was easier to be pissed inside the tent and falling out, than pissing outside the tent and falling in.

The whole day was an enormous pageant of equine admiration, and a fitting tribute to amnesia.

The huge crowd departed in good order, and even better humour, not easy when you're on your hands and knees. They departed in limousines and taxis, coaches, vans and buses. I left in a coma. I didn't bet a winner, but oddly, can't remember parting with any money, either for drinks, food, plasma, or anything else. I did however pay for Irish hospitality. I had a hangover until Easter.

We entered the quiz league, Kevin Quinn, Denis Adams, Paul the bookie, 'Blanders' Blandford, and myself. We repaid Paddy for his faith in us, and restored the good name of the 'Halfway' by becoming joint-winners of the first division of the league; with the "Sebright Arms." We came second the next year, then, as is the way with all teams, we split up and reformed with different constituent parts. For a few seasons I found myself almost a 'mercenary', playing with and for, several pubs around the town. In no particular order of merit, here are pictures of some of them.

The 'Vauxhall Inn', where, by a clever organising process, Quiz and Darts night's coincided, in the same room. We found ourselves sitting, facing our opposition, across the 'flight path', while the home side were practising, or 'throwing up', as it's colourfully known. With the darts whistling through the air between us, it was easy to understand visiting side's dislike of our venue. Nervous tension and downright fear proved to be two contributing factors to our unbeaten season, and God knows what effect the 'arrows' had on the opposition. For a winter season, there was a corner of Rainbow Hill that was forever Agincourt.

The 'Alma', who were genuinely glad to have us. It was a good local, that had fallen on hard times, after a series of hopeless 'new managers' had reduced the place to an atmospheric desert. Our team and scorer immediately doubled the usual Sunday night customer turn-out. The pub mood improved by leaps and bounds, and interest in the games began to grow, as the season progressed. Come the evening of the last match, the place was quite packed out. Amazing. We won the second division title and the guv'nor was moved to buy us all a round of drinks. As he was of the homosexual persuasion, gay abandon could be accurately stated as breaking out.

Mind you, I think the last time the 'Alma' won anything, it was a signed picture of Lord Cardigan, in the fund-raising raffle for Crimean

War canon-balls.

The 'Hereford House' was a place of character and was full of them. An old Bromsgrovian friend of mine and his wife had taken it over, and we were pleased to share his company and his excellent Marston's beer, for a couple of seasons. It was a proper city house, with crib, darts, and pool teams, and we fitted into the general scheme of things nicely. Vic, the gaffer, was a warm and likeable man, and a genuine community spirit was always present; except for Bill, the one-armed bandit. He was the pub know-all. Whatever you'd done, Bill had topped it. My mate said that if you told him you'd talked with the Queen, Bill would have said he'd shagged her. There was no way you could get the better of him. He could out-talk you, drive faster, drink you under the table, and beat you at pool with one arm tied behind his back. Well, actually, he didn't need to tie one behind his back, because he'd only got one arm.

One evening, waiting for some of the team to turn up, listening to this braggard raving on in the pool room, I stupidly challenged him to a game. I think the last straw had been listening to him describing his latest acquisition, a Croix de Guerre medal, (he was an avid War memorabilia collector), and pronouncing it thus 'crux de gurry'.

I was a decent pool player, but I made the fatal mistake of half feeling sorry for him, and underestimating him. I was also paying far too much attention to his cuing action, whereby he tucked the stick into his side with his elbow, and struck the ball with the cue, with his one hand about a foot from the tip.

We'd both sunk a couple of balls, when, too late, I realised the bastard really played rather well. The table had opened up and he zipped round for his shots like Alex Higgins. To my horror he cleaned up. I'd been beaten by a one-armed man; not any old one-armed man, but Bill, the boasting maestro of old Worcester town.

Quiz question in the sporting category: who was the only man to be beaten at pool by a Uni-dexter? Answer: Bruce 'Nobhead' Neath. What a disaster, I had visions of him bawling out the result, as he toured Worcester with a megaphone, in an open-topped car.

It wasn't quite that bad, but as Bill drank in almost all the town's pub's, I think it's a safe bet that only about 25000 of the city's population know the outcome of that awful match. But I'm, sure he didn't know what was the capital of Dahomey.

A short stay at the 'Feathers' in the town, and then with the team settling down as a compact unit, we arrived at the 'Vine'

Merve, 'Jimbo', 'Bunny' and 'Rodders'. Ombersley Road's answer to 'Rainbow'. Actually, not a cuddly bunch at all, but as ruthless a gathering of born-to-be winners, as you could wish to fall foul of.

For a few seasons the league really kept the pubs in and around Worcester, buzzing, on what had been pretty dreary Sunday evenings. What began as a pleasant, friendly, diversion, morphed in turns through good natured competition, earnest rivalry, stern confrontation and, eventually, bitter, spiteful, merciless warfare. No quarter was asked, or given. It was a great fun way to spend an evening. But that's the nature of high level competitive activity of any sort. What was unique to the quiz was how consuming it became. The nights of getting on every buggers nerves in the bar, people passing by muttering "Helena is the state capital of Montana", trying to remember that all Italy's dictators are named after biscuits, turning up with your shirt on, over your pullover. You also got to meet some interesting people, and visit some very strange places. The adjectives in that sentence are inter-changeable.

Jim Gerring, our sport and state capital ace, suffered a very nasty accident to the head, and although he fully recovered, it did tend to play tricks on his memory. He was on heavy medication for a while, and whilst collecting yet another prescription, was asked the usual routine questions; "Name?" "Jim Gerring", "Address?" "24 Cope Road", "Wife's name?" "Oh God, hang on, it'll come to me", "You mean you can't remember the name of your wife, Mr. Gerring?" "Well, I'm sure it starts with a J."

What do they say, 'keep taking the tablets'.

Sad to say, cheating was rife and extremely sophisticated. Most teams pursued it as an art-form some had developed it to a science. Everybody knew it was endemic, but being academically stimulated, we all appreciated our opponent's ingenuity, and were spurred on to even greater acts of duplicity.

On Sunday evenings, our match venue, the assembly-room upstairs at the Vine, owed more to Fagin's den on a handkerchief stealing, training session, than the crucible of high-minded endeavour.

The acts of deception were boundless. One team had mastered the morse-code, and during the individual rounds, the captain would tap out his colleague's answers with his pencil, whilst all the time, looking about him, with a bored facial expression. Another had a team member who could write in tiny, but legible script, with a half-inch long stub of pencil, cupped, and invisible, in the palm of his hand. He would then expertly flick these snowflakes of information across to his team-mates.

Wives and girlfriends wandered into the room, bringing the family dog, whose faithful lope to his master would bring not only a pat and an affectionate cuddle, but a transfer of information, on a missive hidden below his collar.

Teams ran relays downstairs to the toilets, pausing in the bar to garner answers to the general rounds, before racing back to their tables, urine-free, but laden with valuable knowledge.

Clues and answers were secreted in cigarette packets, match-boxes, on shirt-cuffs, palms of hands, under bracelets, inside spectacle-cases, and once, ingeniously, in a set of dentures.

For most of the league's duration, the question setter was my old friend, Derek Woodall. Discussing the cheating phenomena, he remarked, "Compared to this, cracking the Enigma code was a piece of piss."

But it wasn't all about cheating, no by God, it was about winning; by fair means, and not often, but sometimes, disappointingly true, by foul.

The 'Vine' won the league twice, which meant we could cheat with the best, and worst of them, but also meant we knew more than they did about Italian opera, the English monarchy, fifties rock n' roll, Burt Lancaster's film career, formula one motor racing, and once famously, to win the League Cup on a tie-breaker, the Cha-Cha dance champion of 1956. It was Bruce Lee, the better-known Kung-Fu icon.

I've got a cabinet at home, full of pretty ghastly looking trophies, the tangible rewards, and proof of all those seasons. The different dates and pub names, keep the faces and the memories of all our team members, fresh in my mind.

Our team apogee came in our last two seasons at the Vine. I thank all the boys for those outrageous, tense, wonderfully funny, emotional nights. Bob Cummins the guv'nor, would lead off the sing-song that always echoed through the late night, smoke-filled room, "The lights of

Old Aberdeen". Well, he was a Scot, I suppose.

Then the alcohol drenched, sing along Sunday would pump along with 'That'll be the day', 'Oh Boy', 'I'm ready'; Johnny Jones with 'Mule Train', Bunny with the entire Eagles repertoire if you didn't stop him, then taking a line each, and all finishing, sometimes together, the team anthem by the Everly Brothers; 'All I have to do is Dream......"

CHAPTER TWENTY THREE

You Throw It, I'll Catch It

The tours always started the same way. A straggling, multilateral arrival of an unsavoury looking bunch of travellers, heavy laden with crates, cartons, carrier bags, and to add a touch, perhaps the only touch, of sophistication, cool boxes.

Together with the appalling fumes of last night's beer intake, there was always tension in the air. The tension, whose nativity was experience, as we waited and wondered, as we had so often in the past, 'would the bus-driver turn up?' and more pertinent, would he have the bus with him. Then, an audible relief, as the minibus chugged onto the car park, Tesco and Sainsbury's mobile life-support systems were stowed in the redundant luggage hold, and the motley crew stumbled aboard.

"No drinking 'til we've crossed running water." Even at six, or maybe seven, in the morning, there had to be discipline and the team-leader of the day was quick to stamp his authority on the party.

However, the bus was always full of dowsers, all ready, willing, and if not fully able, available with willow-wand and ordnance survey map, to discover that elusive tinkling stream, to release the modest, shy, ring pull, and bring the day's first embalming fluid to it's twitching, bleary-eyed recipient. But just in case our route failed to take us either across the Severn, or the Barbourne Brook, which could be reached in about two minutes, somebody always walked, dick in hand, pissing, across the buses path; It saved a lot of time and earnest geographical argument.

The British are an inventive nation, thanks be given, but we all needed a drink after that early morning display.

So here we all were, early morning, last night in our head, 'England 'til I die', genuine and original, on the road, rugby union, egg-chaser aficionado's; bucketing down the road we hoped would lead, in the fullness of time and on a higher alcoholic astral plane, to Twickenham.

The journey wasn't always via the same route, but it was always the same. Everybody knew the way, except the driver. In a bus full of people, bonded together with the glorious English language, he was the only one who could speak it, but not understand it.

"I said fucking left at the island, not fucking right."

"You didn't say which fucking left though, did you cully?"

The scene was set for several hours of rapier wit and sparkling repartee, in similar, and occasionally, even more graphic mode. Thank God the bar was now fully open. We had a long day ahead of us; we hadn't got out of Worcester yet.

We were a job-lot of artisans, predominately Royal Mail's finest, but things were very different when we entered the jolly japester world of the travelling professional classes.

On a tour of Paris with Gloucester Rugby Club, Dennis Adams and I found our progress to our seats blocked by a well-dressed solicitor from 'the city', wedged, paralytically drunk, on the floor between two of the back seats on the upper deck of the coach. It was 5.30 a.m. He was a big bloke, wearing an even bigger Crombie over-coat. He was on the floor, still sucking on a half-empty whiskey bottle and whimpering like a pissed-up puppy. He wallowed in slopping beer dregs and the Crombie was sucking up the booze like a sponge; he was recycling his own urine, and occasional stutters of manic laughter convinced us he thought it was all good fun.

With not only two nation's road systems, but also the English Channel yet to be negotiated, here truly, was a man at ease with himself. As we clambered over him, a ripple of stale beer ran round his nostrils, as the bus braked sharply. It occurred to us he might drown. 'Fuck him' we thought, and relaxed in our seats.

The Kingsholm faithful had settled into 'drink a can a beer a mile' mode, and the party games were in full swing. 'Forfeits, when played by grown men who would be declared clinically dead, except for the fact that they could still open a bottle and get the smaller end of it inside their mouth, can be an interesting spectacle, for a spectator.

Two of the solicitor's fellow peddlers of the law had progressed to the grand final, leaving in their wake a coterie of broken drunkards, all of whom had fallen at earlier hurdles, like having to eat their own index fingers, or abseil out of the quarter-light windows of the coach. Having successfully ingested a full bottle of Alka-Seltzer, after his colleague had been shaking it up for five minutes, mad lawyer number one was certain victory was his, when he announced mad lawyer number two would never despatch a lollipop to deny him the title. With the beatific smile possessed only by the divine and the walking dead-drunk, he produced the confection, a six-inch diameter glazed lolly on a two-foot, quarter inch square, wooden stick. His timber-eating colleague had proved him wrong and wolfed the lot, prior to reaching the M4.

Before we arrived at the quaintly named comfort stop, or, in the case of the 'Cherry and White' army, made a shambolic, leering, foul-mouthed attack on the public conveniences at Leigh Delamere Motorway services, things on the upper deck were getting interesting.

With his successful impression of the Thames Barrier denying the spilt and regurgitated alcohol any escape, the upstairs floor was now two or three inches deep in Tetleys. The sea of booze ran under the seats and splashed up the sides of the Coach. Every acceleration sent the tidal wave down to 'Crombie Man', and threatened to drive him down the back stairway. Each time the driver braked, the whole, seething mass roared to the front and smashed its way several feet up the panoramic windscreen.

The beer-crates had been lifted on to the seats and we all sat on the back-rests, watching the Crombie king's catatonic battle for survival in the mild and bitter aquarium. Suddenly he spluttered into life: it was when the tide was out, as it were, and the realisation hit him that he was no longer having a drink, but more, the drink was now having him.

As the bus lurched forward, the sight of this wall of foul alcohol, carrying its surfing cigarette ends, roaring like the Severn Bore, down the aisle to meet him, invested in him, the power to stagger wildly to his feet. He stood like a bison in a thunderstorm, soaked, his crombie dripping, as the deluge swept ankle-high beneath him, and cascaded, thundering down the stairs.

I will not dwell on the ensuing melee, suffice for me to offer a travel tip: If you ever travel on a Rugby Tour double deck coach, make sure you book your seats upstairs, at the front.

Footnote to this story; rugby supporters of all persuasion are generally a friendly, gregarious breed, but most unusually the upstairs and downstairs factions of that particular tour never did manage to cohabit peacefully.

Second footnote; 'Crombies' mates obviously still in prankish mood, threw all his clothes and his shoes, into the sea, as we ploughed across from Portsmouth to Le Havre. They did leave him his coat, but only, I suspect, because it was too sodden and heavy to lift.

He appeared for breakfast in coat only, still leaving a dribbling black and yellow trail. Quite what the proper holidaying passengers must have thought of this almost naked, incontinent wild man, can only be imagined.

On the morning of the match, Dennis and I made our way by stages and bars, to the environs of the Parc des Princes. Close by the ground we pitched up at a pleasant, bustling café, and drank our brandies and coffees, whilst the trampling hordes made their way to the scene of the impending violence. We sat on the pavement and cheered, and were cheered by, fellow 'Glos' supporters as they bore their banners and scarves towards the ground.

Then, out of the throng, striding purposefully and barefoot, came Crombie man. He wore the stinking mantle that was once his coat with pride, now a little drier, but attracting a squadron of French flies in close formation. He waved and proffered a cheerful 'Morning chaps, lets give those frogs a seeing to' then disappeared into the surging mass. He looked and sounded, in excellent spirits. In every way, a real 'Glawster boy'.

The Parc; a cavernous bowl, a cacophony reverberating round and through, the concrete rib-cage of the stadium. The crowd, cheering, jeering, roaring, groaning.

Saxophones, trumpets, drummers and the wonderful Dax band. A cockerel struts before the sea of waving flags. The blue shirts appear; uproar. The whites of England gingerly enter the cauldron; hoots of derision.

This is the Parc, this is Le Rugby, this is France.

"In quietness and in confidence shall be your strength."

England lost a heart-breaking game 10 points to 9.

It was Will Carlings first game for England.

In his career as player and captain of England,

He would never lose another game to the French.

To Twickenham, to see the 'new' South Africans, back in the fold after their years of apartheid isolation. England selected two Nigerians, Victor Ubogu and Steve Ojomoh in their starting line-up. There was not a black face to be seen in the Springbok selection, so no change there then. Travelling down; another three hour exchange of expletives with our driver, visits to several unknown villages, down many unmarked by-roads, and by way of the occasional gated lane, we arrived, by the grace of God, in Stokenchurch, bang on opening time at the pub on the village green, beloved of all egg-chasers, and particularly Gloucester boys.

A diet of Guinness, with Stella mixers, insured that levels of interest, conversation, and blood pressure were all rising nicely, as we took our seats in the back garden area of the pub. The temperature was comfortable, the beer was drinkable, the sky was blue, the driver had stopped screaming, we might yet get to Twickers without committing murder, or travelling in by train. A pleasant, gentle hum of inebriated, good humoured banter wafted across the air; then the miracle of Buckinghamshire occurred.

Like a sting in the corner of the eye, a black shadow appeared, then was gone. I turned and looked skyward; two more shapes cut across the sun, dipping and turning, pirouetting, flashing and soaring into the heavens. Above them others were arriving, circling high above, gently cruising down to lower altitude, augmenting the gymnastic display as they lit the sky with avian pyrotechnics. Red kites, controlling their breath-taking flights with long, forked tails, dropping to the tables to take left-over sandwiches, lonely crisps. The birds had been common scavengers in London's filthy medieval streets, but how wonderful to see them here, in their brilliant acrobatic glory. No doubt they'd take your misplaced scarf or handkerchief too, as Shakespeare noted, "when the kite builds, look to lesser linen."

It's possible to see them now, whilst driving down the M40 to London, all the way from High Wycombe, almost to the M25. Since the introduction of half a dozen pairs in the Chiltern Hills some ten years ago, they are now thriving and have adapted easily to modern motorised life. How long before that unmistakable silhouette is seen against London's skyline once again?

Ennobled mentally and spiritually, we pressed on to Twickers and were pleased to note the Springboks side included the last of the 'old brigade' of players, Danny Gerber, the flying winger, and the incomparable Naas Botha, the fly half who was an inspiration to generations of players, from all over the Rugby World. "Pace and Grace".

My friend Howard Jones and I, found ourselves sitting high up in the stand, behind the south goalposts. We were two English supporters in a wedge of about two hundred South Africans. Never famed for their modesty, we were subjected to a continual lambasting, as the 'boks opened up in fine style, culminating in a well-worked try, to give them an early lead. "You're on the rack now", screamed a devotee. Mercifully, England regained their composure and began to control the game. Just before the interval Rory Underwood dived over the line between the posts, immediately below us. "Whose on the fucking rack now then?" exhorted Howard. The response was a stunned and ominous silence. "It's going to be interesting at half-time" I remarked to 'H'.

Surprisingly the Rainbow Warriors took it on the chin and, after a deserved England victory, actually congratulated us. 'Christ, that was a close call' I remember thinking.

On another Twickers' day when Howard had left me holding his beer, so that he might have a few words with his and, I suppose, everyone's favourite player, Gareth Edwards, who was walking through the West car park, I also met an old and respected friend.

Climbing the stairs to our seats in the North stand, I found myself adjacent to my old friend Lord Longford. "Good afternoon my Lord, I trust the game will be a good one." "Er, yes, so do I" "It's wonderful, is it not, to see the Welsh team recovering from their days in the doldrums" "Er, yes, I think so" "Well, do enjoy your day Sir, its been grand to see you again, after such a long time." "Er, yes, good to see you too."

Howard was wide-eyed and open-mouthed; "You bastard, I never knew you knew Lord Longford." "Who in the name of Myra Hindley was that oik", must have mused the peer.

The sighting of Gareth Edwards reminds me of the story of the Welsh team, when the 'prince of centres' Barry John was his half back partner, walking out onto Cardiff Arms Park, and discussing, for the first time, the team's tactics for the day. "What's our game plan then boy, what's our strategy?" asked Edwards. "You throw it and I'll catch it" replied John.

In today's game, where not only does every player appear to have an individual special 'coach', and every tiniest move is detailed and choreographed, how refreshing and amazing, to realise that those two great players, in possibly Wales' greatest team, did everything by instinct, their natural flair driving the entire fifteen to emulate them.

Through most of our intense rugby watching days, the Welsh team was at perhaps the lowest ebb in its history, and Howard had to endure a series of gut-wrenching defeats, both in the five nations' championships and across the world. I spent many such days in his company and he was forever gracious in defeat, and magnanimous in victory. Honest and fair-minded, and knowledgeable about the game, he never faltered in his support for the Scarlets, nor detracted from the victors. An honourable friend, and a true sportsman.

Pork pies and Tetleys, chicken legs and wine (no, not a Cliff Richard Christmas record), but the après-ski nosh-up on the way back.

The bus rattled home through the early evening gloaming; after a few more 'refreshers', the company moved to show their vocal skills, to the accompaniment of 'Blind Davy' Rice's moving harmonica riffs. Perhaps a romp through the Buddy Holly song-book, or a sing-along with the Travelling Wilbury's. It might have been melodic cacophony, but it was our melodic cacophony.

One evening, after aircraft-spotting at Heathrow airport (never let it be said the boys had no other outside interests), we somehow managed to roll into a welcoming country pub, on the outskirts of Stow on the Wold. We sallied in, bought in a few double rounds, and were soon in full choral mode with our Rugby songs for Swingin' Lovers collection. The guv'nor was a large, friendly cove, and decided to take us on, 'bob a nob', with his in-house choral team. Erstwhile huntin', shootin', and hangin' types, and their blue-stocking ladies, began to belt out 'Eskimo Nell' and other lullabies, in full unexpurgated glory. This country set could more than hold their own, and I fancy, quite often held someone else's, and gave it full throttle in the filth and obscenity department. I revised my opinion, they were the huntin', shootin', and shaggin' set.

The ribald debauchery continued long after kicking-out time, when sadly we had to leave this temple of self-denial, all the more understanding of each others life-styles, and all with a much expanded vocabulary of heinous and more than disgusting anglo-saxon metaphors for copulation.

A good night was had by all, don't ya know.

The Millennium Stadium in Cardiff replaced an earlier concrete structure, based, I always thought on the Parc in Paris. Both had towering terraces of cold stone, and if your seat was anywhere near the top tier, it was prudent to buy a sturdy length of rope, crampons, and a bottle of anti-vertigo tablets. Such was the elevation, it looked and felt, that if you had leant forward, in the top seats behind the goal-posts, you could have rested your elbows on the top of them.

French and Welsh Rugby at its best, has much in common, especially in the back play. The difference, and quite often the deciding factor for victory, especially of late, has been the French superiority in the forwards.

Their power-house production line for these brutally effective front eight players, has always been the South West of France, in Toulouse, Perpignon, Pau and Biarritz. Coincidentally, the English game has also drawn its most outstanding forwards from the same geographical area of England, in Bath, Bristol and Gloucester.

Phillipe Saint Andre, the meteoric wing and one-time captain of France, knew all about this, and was a great influence in developing fluent, running back play, to complement a sturdy pack of forwards, when he was in charge at Gloucester. He used to say "The forwards carry the piano, the backs play it." To continue the musical analogy, the other ingredient in Gallic football has always been the volatile temperament, and quite often a game involving the French, has regularly drawn comparisons to Beethoven's Eroica and Chopin's Funeral March, both during the same eighty minutes.

Whilst Foghorn Leghorn struts his stuff in Paris, Billy the goat keeps the Royal Regiment of Wales in good order in Cardiff. Then the nation's sympathies diverge. Foghorn becomes a tasty coq au vin, whilst Billy retires to Brecon Barracks, to have his hooves manicured, and his horns buffed up, in pampered retirement;
"See the conquering hero comes,
Sound the trumpets, beat the drums."
The French add another line, "warm the oven, peel the plums."
The great glory of the Millennium is the music, the songs.
The aerodynamics of the amphitheatre, let the soaring sounds roll around the terraces, up under the roof, then out and across the ground, to meet and rise, across the playing area. 'We'll keep a Welcome', 'Calon

Lan', 'Men of Harlech', 'Cwm Rhondda', and of course 'Hen Wlad Fy Nhadau'.

Raw emotion, mystery and mystique. How can Wales ever lose in Cardiff, with seventy thousand voices raised in surging harmonies of triumphal adulation?

The crowd is, and always has been, not an addition, but a vital living part of the national game, the national psyche. The land of song is the land of their fathers. It belongs to all and should be rejoiced by all. I think the magic is diminished, if these great traditional anthems are taken from the crowd, and offered up by 'stars' of the celebrity world, however pretty and articulate they may be. In the dying moments of a mighty contest, those seventy thousand voices can drive Wales over for a try to seal the victory. Katherine Jenkins can't.

The French in contrast, have only one great battle cry, 'La Marseillaise', but what a blood-boiling, irresistible call to the colours it is. Away from home and outnumbered, the song still wafts the smell of cordite into the opposition dressing room, and prickles the scalp of the sternest, alien, patriot. "Aux armes, citoyens!" We are ready.

The two nations have fought out many unforgettable matches, where both sides have played to a standstill, the result undecided until the final whistle. There is a strong feeling of mutual respect and appreciation. Vive la difference. If patriotism is indeed the last refuge of a scoundrel, then, in my opinion, it is a refuge full of true rugby followers, and one I would gladly retire to.

I have one glowing memory of a visit to the Welsh capital, when we broke our outward journey, for rest and refreshment, at Tintern Abbey. 'Steady Eddie' drove us effortlessly down to the site of the once powerful Abbey church, sitting on a lush green pasture, cradled in the arms of the slowly winding River Wye.

Howard summoned up a wondrous table of culinary delights, supplemented by a mouth watering selection of fine wines supplied by 'Bob the Dog'. I had latterly come to know Bob, a refugee from the North East, possessing the easy going, good natured demeanour of his peers, and also the dry and incisive wit associated with that part of the world. Any man with such characteristics, who also knew his Sauvignon from his Muscadet, was bound to be a friend of mine forever.

We sat beneath the skeletal shadow of the great gothic Cistercian church, on a manicured lawn that had once been the main body of the building. A gentle, warming wind pulled the cotton-wool clouds across the towering sky. They moved lazily between the roofless walls, past what would have been the great west window, whilst the Wye rolled lazily down to its tryst with the Severn.

It was wondrously silent, save the warbling song of the skylark, ascending, as Wordsworth's "ethereal minstrel." The clamour of battle, still to come, just a few miles down the valley, seemed a million miles away. I thought of Henry the Fifth and his little army, on that last still night, watching the fires burning on the horizon, before Agincourt. This day men of Monmouth were again readying themselves for the contest; but this time not with, but against, the English.

Ireland and the Irish, are of course, something quite different.

An ever darkening winter sky, as I drive with Howard, Dennis and Kevin, up the tortuous road, laughingly designated the A5. The sleet turns to snow, as we somehow pass Llangollen, even the street lights seem afraid of the dark up here. The weather gets worse, I detect black ice on the road, the car splutters, but carries on, the windscreen wipers appear on the verge of giving up the battle against the growing snowflakes, the boys are all asleep, we had a few at Paddy's 'Halfway House' before we set off. I mean, they had a few, I just had the one. Never mind, Dennis had kindly brought his new tape for me to play whilst I somehow kept the Ford Sierra on the straight, and definitely, bloody narrow, highway to Holyhead. Through the spasmodic honking and snoring, I'm playing it now; Chris Rea's "Road to Hell". I decide to have a serious conversation with Dennis when, or if, we ever get to the port, on the place of irony in a pissed-up, fast asleep, wit-frightening, drive to the last place God ever created in the universe.

I'm wondering whether I should play a joke on them, turn the car round, and slip-slide my way back to Worcester; pull up outside the 'Halfway' and shout, "Here we are boys, get your tickets ready, I'm fucking off home." The idea is beginning to sound attractive, when I realise I'm crossing the causeway to Holy Island, thereupon lies the magical Holyhead. We're here. Well, it wasn't so bad, I've only had white knuckles and a headache for four hours, and my eyes couldn't feel any hotter, if the proverbial hot pointed stick had been used upon my viewing organs.

Park up, embark; I'm with an army of shouting, beer-fuelled party people, who want to piss it up all the way to Dun Loaghaire. They're at least ten pints in front of my passengers, and a good fifteen in front of me; this always makes for a definite difference of opinion on the merits of speed-spewing, fighting on the floor, and marathon silly song contests. Although the bar is open day and night, I hope they won't be able to keep the uproar going. They do it in style.

It's one of life's deepest mysteries, when you're sober, and rowdy bastards who are manically pissed, keep you up all night, come the dawn, you are the wrecked and hopeless case, pleading only for a place to put your head and sleep, whilst they step out into the burgeoning light, happy, bouncy, frighteningly fit, and raring to go into the next drinkathon.

I stepped off the boat and onto Ireland's green and pleasant land. I felt like a bag of shit; I wanted to sleep for at least three days, I looked at my watch, "fucking hell, the match starts in five hours time." I kept a straight face, but inside me, I could hear myself crying.

Kevin Quinn was our team leader. Kev was from Galway, and his brothers were coming up to meet us. It sounded less like a reunion and more like Gunfight at the O'Connell corral. His cousin met us at the dock in a Garda police car, he hadn't stolen it, he was a member of that august force. He greeted Kevin and all of us warmly, and said "You've had a long night and a rough, noisy passage, with all those ignorant English bastards, so I've got you a nice hotel to chill out in; have a nice relaxing bath, grab yourselves a bit of shut-eye, I'll give you a ring and pick you all up later."

Thank the Lord. Sleep; heavenly.

Twenty minutes later there was a knock on the door, I pulled my jeans on, forgot my socks, stumbled out into Dublin daylight; we were on the town, pre-match style.

We rolled down O'Connell Street in the Garda car, it was warm and sunny. We did a bit of shopping and I bought a lovely piece of Waterford crystal for my wife. We saw the 'Floozy in the Jaccuzi', and then clocked in to the rendezvous bar with Kev's Galway brothers. I had drawn my last sober breath on Irish soil.

The brothers were big, powerful looking boys. They wore matching tweed jackets, with matching broken noses, and raging, wayward ginger hair. They told us we had tickets next to them, and about seven thousand other Ireland supporters, on the huge, uncovered East Terrace. Unpatriotically, I remember thinking, "I hope to fuck England don't win."

Kev's cousin hid the Garda car behind one of O'Connell Street's many hotels, and together, the wayward policeman, Kev and the Galway boys, and the English bastards, began the long amnesiac lurch to Lansdown Road.

After what seemed like an eternity, with my sockless feet rubbing against my shoes, stumbling, bumping, barging and falling, head banging, knee grazing, elbow bruising and cursing, we were queuing to enter the wonderful, ramshackle glory that was the headquarters of the Irish Rugby Union.

Notwithstanding the awe-inspiring sea of tricolours, forty thousand voices wheeling Molly Malone's wheel barrow round and round the quaking timbers of the old stands, and an atmospheric patina of exhaled Guinness fumes, thick and strong enough to render the Catholic Marching Band pissed at a thousand paces, two things stood out in my mind, unique to any rugby ground.

One, they'd built a timber-framed house in the ground, just behind the corner flag to the right hand side of the West Terrace, and two, even more interestingly, a railway ran right through the stadium.

I had time to ponder these wondrous novelties, as we stood, hundreds deep, with seemingly the entire population of Dublin pressing us forward, at the level crossing which served as entrance to the ground.

A train appeared, thundered past us, and disappeared under the main stand. Being almost in an alcoholic 'out of body' state, it was a surreal, kafka-esque moment. Bells rang, lights flashed green, the barriers lifted, the one and only ticket examiner shouted, "have you'ze all got yer feckin' tickets?" We all shouted "Yes!" and 40,000 people entered the ground.

Not only was this the epitome of crowd-control, but what a feckin' way to run a railway.

The timber framed house, incidentally, is the clubhouse of 'The Wanderers' Ireland's oldest and senior club. They had the run of

Lansdown Road, much as Harlequins used to play home matches at Twickenham.

We stood and sang together, and the rain began to fall. There was no cover on the terraces, but nobody cared. I'd changed scarves with my Quinn brother even before the kick-off, and we were all getting on famously. It was a pulsating game, and when Ireland scored a scintillating try early in the second half, my new friend punched me joyously in the stomach. I was only unconscious for a few minutes, but my stomach was telling me, 'don't let Ireland score again, please'.

Irish arias and rebel songs resonated through the crowd, followed by a non-stop stream of hot dogs and Guinness. I lost the feeling in both my legs; England won. Somebody had to tell me the result, I didn't see nor remember the rest of the second half.

Next things we were queuing yet again at the level-crossing, bells again rang, lights flashed, a train blurred past and we were swept out of the ground into the ever open arms of Dublin's hospitality. I was beginning to think that the 'hospital' part of that word was going to come in handy pretty soon. It was only 5.30pm, but I'd been awake for thirty five hours. I already felt like the good time that had been had by all.

Our police-car chauffeur, slammed us round the city nightspots, parking wherever he liked, and gaining instant access to all the interesting venues.

I no longer had any concept of time and had lost the sense of taste; I had somehow chomped my way through a doner kebab, that tasted suspiciously like a Guinness sandwich, and when even my cigarettes had the tang of the black stuff about them, I decided to give up the habit.

My next recollection is of a smoke-filled, music-thumping, strobe-light flashing room, with walls, the ceiling, and even the floor, made of glass. I was surrounded by dozens of images of myself; confused and disorientated, I was lost in this prism prison. It was a nightmare.

A pleasant Dublin girl asked me to dance; I slipped and crashed into one of the ever colour-changing wall panels. Through the haze, she and all her other images, melted away.

Howard was dancing with several other differently lit Howard's, and chatting seductively to most of them. I tried to drag him from the floor, before he exchanged telephone numbers. Night turned into very late night, then into very early morning.

My hands and feet were numb, my heart appeared to be the only internal organ of my body still functioning, and threatening to stop at any moment. I'd lost the ability to speak and was sleeping with my eyes open.

It was a Dublin miracle that somehow, we all woke up in the same hotel, later that day. The full Irish breakfast of Guinness, fried Guinness, baked Guinness, black pudding and mushrooms, fortified us for the final punishing day of fun and games in the Emerald Isle.

Our Garda taxi duly arrived, and leaving the city on the northern side, we were whisked away, in what seemed like no time at all, to the wonderful little fishing village of Howth.

The Irish name for Dublin is Baile Atha Cliath, which, generously translated, is Blackpool. That being so, then Howth is it's Lytham St. Annes.

This pretty settlement with its white stone houses, and natural, boat-filled harbour, is just a few miles, and a whole world away, from Ireland's capital city.

It was a warm, sunny morning, and we all sat, Guinness in hand, outside the sturdy village pub, just across from the breakwater. The boats rose and fell with the easy lapping tide, bees buzzed about their business in the trellis-climbing honeysuckle, and I was beginning to come back to life. This unspoilt place, evocative of Devon fishing ports of my boyhood days, inhabits still, a warm place in my memory, and will always do so.

Another round of the staff of Irish life, and then back to Kev's cousins' for lunch.

His wife welcomed us all, and we sat at the table, where a fine Irish lace cloth supported a full silver service and an impressive candelabra. By the time the wine was chasing the sumptuous roast dinner, conversation rang round the room, it felt as though we'd known each other all our lives.

One last ride in the Garda taxi down to Dun Laoghaire, and after warm and tearful goodbyes, onto the Holyhead ferry. Mercifully, it was a calm crossing and apart from the unavoidable presence on the boat, of about two hundred manic funsters, dressed as court jesters, complete with multi-belled caps, and faces on sticks, an uneventful one.

With the background of these snoring, belching, floor-twitching grotesques, sleep was out of the question, and eventually we slid gently into the dying light of Holy Island's evening.

A mantle of snow lay over Snowdonia, there was a tangible coolness in the air, and a dull pain behind all our eyes, heralded our return from the land of Irish make-believe.

As night began to envelope the quayside, the weary troops began to disembark, their regimental colours carried around their necks; Gloucester, Bath, Leicester, Harlequins, Northampton, Richmond, Wasps. All had been called, most had managed to return. Car engines coughed into life, headlights pierced the darkness, and the long road home stretched out ahead of us.

The Dublin campaign was over; at least for another two years.

CHAPTER TWENTY FOUR

Sylvestor

I really like the story about the honest, straight-forward, working class bloke, watching the emotionally climactic moments in the film 'Brief Encounter', between Trevor Howard and Celia Johnson. Both racked with angst, guilt and stifling self-denial, the scene staggers hopelessly, impossibly on: "Please darling, say you will", "O Alec, I can't, you know I can't" "But darling, just this one moment, we must", "It's just not possible, we dare not, there's so much at stake". "Darling forget all that, it's just about us now ….." "Oh Alec, I'm so afraid ……"

At this point, working class bloke had just about had enough, "For God's sake, give 'er one" he shouted from the stalls.

My association with Sylvestor has absolutely nothing to do with this scenario, but I thought it would be a more interesting opening to the chapter, about how I came to possess a stuffed cartoon-character cat.

The day had started, as in retrospect, so many seem to have done, in a bar adjacent to a railway station. In fact, this bar was the 'King and Castle' and was actually inside a railway station, Kidderminster Town, on the Severn Valley Railway. My friend Richard and I had engaged ourselves in the laudable task of liberating several pints of Bathams bitter, from the dark cellar confinement in which they had been imprisoned. As another of my philosophical side-kicks is wont to say, "After all the brewer's trouble, we owe it to him and his ilk, not to let the beer go bad." The wonderful elixir was going down effortlessly, and warmth, benevolence and bonhomie, the three horsemen of the paralysis, were dancing on the table between our glasses.

However, just when it appeared that another afternoon on the Batham's 'slow stopper', calling at all stations; Myopia, Dyslexia, Amnesia, and Stumbling in the Street, was on the cards, fate, in the form of an advertising 'flyer', intervened. It appeared that today was Hampton Loade Station Gala Day. We decided to travel up the line to support this noble cause, and put some money in the kitty for those splendid volunteers, who kept the old station in immaculate condition, working tirelessly, and of course, for no financial reward.

We drained our glasses and shuffled out on to the concourse. I heard a muffled sound, from somewhere deep within me. It was my liver, whispering "Thank the Lord of human organs for that."

It was a bright summer's day, and we chuffed our way gently up the lovely Severn Valley, in our 1930 vintage 'time capsule', Swindon-green pannier tank, complete with a rake of Gresley teak-bodied passenger coaches.

Hampton Loade is a small, quiet village that sits astride the river, and has been a crossing point for centuries. 'Loade' is an old English word denoting a ferry. One family has supplied the ferryman for several generations, and the present incumbent is a sturdy lad, who knows the wiles of the river as of second nature. It's as well that he has this know-how, for his 'ferry boat' resembles nothing so much as an upturned side-panel from a large garden shed, with 'afterthought' benches nailed haphazardly onto each side, for the passengers comfort and delectation. This whole impressive, river-going transportation system, crosses the stream by means of attachment to a steel hawser drag-line, and the ferryman's ability to steer the craft by means of vigorous propulsion with an extended broom handle.

I have to smile each morning, as I pass the village turning, off the main Bridgnorth – Kidderminster road. It now has an additional road sign: 'Hampton Loade ferry, sat-nav error'. Apparently, convoys of articulated juggernauts, driven by non-English speaking Poles, Serbs and Slovaks, have been forging down the narrow, winding lane to the waterside, urged on by their satellite navigational aids (how poignantly ironic is that?), only to be confronted, at water's edge, by ferryman, and 'HMS Outhouse'. We can all of us Worcestershire folk, be thankful for the combination of 'ferry-load-capacity' knowledge, and rampant xenophobia, possessed by the keeper of the crossing, that the river Severn between Hampton and Bewdley is not clogged with half-submerged container lorries, jam-packed with lap-tops, mobile phones and other vital necessities of life in modern Britain.

Hampton Station is an idyllic place. I am always deeply aware of being in England, and of being English, here.

"Such is the patriot's boast, where 'er we roam,
His first, best country ever is, at home."

Standing on the cathedral-quiet platform, only the lazy bees, and flitting, flirting, song birds intrude into the snug, valley reverie. But not today. It's uproar and anoraks day. Everywhere, bearded, unwashed, worshippers of the 'Great God Steam', are delving, diving, digging, tunnelling, into mounds of rampant railwayana. And that's just the ladies of the following. The blokes of the species are ploughing through wheel-barrow loads of magazines, time-tables, hard-back and paper-back books, treaties and dissertations, totems and theories on tramways, name-plates and shed-codes, pictures and paintings, badges and tea-cloths, fish plates and rail-chairs. They are all, like me, continuing the life-time process of converting their pleasant, semi-detached suburban houses into Steptoe and Son's junkyard. Believe me, this is a special breed. They cut across all social classes. They are the only people who own property in this country that is actually depreciating in value.

I've seen the light. I've called a halt. I will buy no more. The urge isn't dead; the need hasn't gone away; it's just that I can only get into my house now by means of a ladder via the back bedroom window. I decided to give a donation, and support the Station Fund Raffle.

I stood in the marquee before the trestle table, and hastily erected sets of shelves, and surveyed the cornucopia of kitsch arrayed before me. Every nook, and most of the crannies, were jammed and rammed with ghastly, garish 'objet non d'art'. Where in God's name does all this tawdry tat come from? Is there a hellish factory of the horrid, perhaps, upon which Leonard Rossiter based his 'Grot' Company, churning out this hallucinatory rubbish? I'll bet the owner, whilst planning his production lines, invented Candy Floss.

I bought a ticket, and was about to turn away, when high up on the top shelf, between the plaster of Paris three-dimensional wall plates, and the 'Little Ballerina' music boxes, I saw him: Sylvestor. As soon as we made eye contact, I knew I must have this exceptional cat. An unseemly episode of bartering occurred, but eventually, after parting with seven pounds, I was united with the fabulous feline. A 'West Country' pacific blasted it's way out of the station bound for Bridgnorth, and clutching my new found talisman to my breast, I was enveloped in the heady cocktail of steam, smoke and beer fumes.

He was mine!

Thus began our enduring odyssey. Since that day Sylvestor has accompanied, and sometimes, taken me, well over 40,000 miles with steam locomotives. He is now a celebrity of sorts on the trains, in the pubs, and alas, some of the jails, across the UK and tracts of the European continent. The "creeping hours" of time, mean that his whiskers are now a little greyer, his tail a little limper, and his nose a smidgeon redder, but Lord knows, that applies to me as well. So we continue our journey of delight, ever celebrating the wonders of steam in the twenty-first century, and the enduring attraction of real ale. It is a source of joy to me, as we travel the rails, to meet, and enjoy the company of, so many warm, friendly, and exceptional new friends.

We've both come a long way together, and I trust we still have a long way to go.

As Sylvestor would, and indeed, does say:

"Sufferin' Succotash!"

Sylvestor and friend in holiday mode

CHAPTER TWENTY FIVE

T.I.T.S
Travel In Trains Society

Patron : Sylvestor
Nostalgia and Rumours Editor : B H Neath
Scandal and Litigation Editor : R Barnes

Our Motto : 'Sufferin' Succotash

T.I.T.S
A new concept in rail travel
Are you one of the many travellers out there,
Unsure of your facts, worried about dates, concerned about timings,
don't know which way to turn?
We feel TITS can help you.

We are here to help.
We are here to listen.
We are here to stand up for you. Is there any other society that holds
its members in such esteem?
We know TITS put them in the shade.

We give you:
Up to the minute tour news, real opinion of tour expectations
Locomotive information
Latest available loco performance news
On-train bar/real ale news
Destination best pub guide
Back-room griff on owners and operators
SP on railway totty

Reach out for T.I.T.S Join our society!!

Join us today and get your free T.I.T.S badge, carry it with you always, because, don't forget every time a fellow member meets you, he will challenge you, "show us your TITS"
Failure to do so renders you liable to buy your comrade a pint.

"We have seen the future, through smoke and steam, and it is Bass best bitter, and intensive care"

B. Neath

The Travel in Trains Society

Tits was formed (or should that be, were formed?) in the Autumn of 2002, by myself and my good friend, Richard Barnes.

Richard had the wholesome vision of a happy band of comrades united in their love of railways, chuffing round the country together, borne up by noble aspiration, remarking on the wonders of the countryside passing by our window, and invoking the finer feelings, and grander inner goodliness of the human condition. Beethoven's Ode to Joy, summarises it perfectly,

"Just as his son's hurtle through

His glorious universes."

I was on nodding terms with most of the steam charter train operators, had an up to date copy of England's Good Pub Guide, a credit card with a few quid left to spend, a mentality oft described as 'crippled' and/or 'insane", and a stuffed cat called Sylvestor.

We felt it was a winning combination, and capable of propelling both us and the embryo society, onto greater things. After all, Hitler had managed to plunge the entire world into global warfare, working from a painter and decorator's shop in downtown Vienna, and he hadn't even got a stuffed cat.

We burnt the midnight oil; we drew up our manifesto, we set out our strategy, we defined our objectives, we bullet-pointed our mission statement.

Then we threw all that bullshit into the waste basket, and I phoned a couple of mates and asked if they wanted to join us. When they were convinced there was no fee, no rules, no plan, and definitely, no initiation ceremony, they said count us in.

We decided our first tour would be to the West Somerset Railway. It was an unqualified success. All four of us got there, all four got back home. Nobody had a fight, no-one ended up in Taunton Jail. Never mind, we all promised we'd do better next time.

I introduced a news-letter, 'Janus, looking back, looking forward.' Is that pseudo nonsense or what? People were looking at me in a new light, one shining directly into my eyes, whilst someone held my head in a vice-like grip. I dropped the name after a couple of issues.

Notwithstanding what I thought was a howling, unfair, criticism of my new-born journal, I took it on the chin, thought "Up yours", and ploughed on. Despite this hiccup, the society prospered, and went from strength to strength, approx 3.7% to 4.5%, say from Tetleys to Old Peculiar; Has the ring of 'From here to Eternity' about it, with perhaps the same conclusion.

We decided that a code of conduct was necessary, so as to portray the society in an acceptable, perhaps even envied light, and agreed, on the subject of drink, that as Dean Martin once said, "You're not drunk if you can lie on the floor without holding on." After all, standards must be maintained.

Our forming of the Old Boys Brigade (over 60's) 1st Worcester, coincided with a sensational programme of steam-hauled tours to Plymouth, over the Devon banks. This firmly established the society, not least in the eyes of the tour operators. Using all of my conversational skills, I talked, long into the night to save the society being banned, and promised not to sing in Welsh, talk in English, or scream in agony. A pattern, it has to be acknowledged, was emerging.

Our two founder members were Andy Brown, the 'Fantom Phireman' of 85A, a one-time worker, and indeed passed fireman at Worcester steam shed in the nineteen fifties, and 'Trackside Trev', Trevor Till, a steam aficionado from way back when, who remembered spotting, in his youth, at Tamworth, and even saw the post-war streamliners in action on the Coronation Scot.

Finally, Sylvestor the cat; he was our mascot, our totem, the reason cited to blame our table for ungentlemanly behaviour. He travels with me always, whether on a Tits outing, or on any other railway journey occasion. He has become an icon; people know that whither goest the cat, so goest I, and avoid the carriage, and if possible the train, like a plague village.

We are, like Cromwell, "Damned to everlasting fame." We exploded on the railway scene; we were travelling everywhere, to Devon, East Anglia, Scotland, the South of England. When there were no available main-line tours, we strutted our ageing stuff around the preserved lines. Heritage travellers on heritage railways. We made more trips than a colony of leaf-carrying ants in a 'build your own ant hill out of leaves' documentary on leaf-carrying ant television.

As our notoriety grew, others begged to join us, if only to become aware of our movements, and avoid us. We signed up 'country members' from Scotland and Ireland. I suppose they really were 'other country members'.

By the end of 2003, we had clocked up some serious mileage, and Trev had sullied his hitherto squeaky-clean reputation, by threatening to stuff a lady of senior years through the quarter-light window, when she made some disparaging remarks about Sylvestor. To many passengers in the carriage, this had been the highlight of our already glorious day out over the Settle and Carlisle line. I went on a main-line steam locomotive driving course in Poland, followed by a week, the first of many, on the rail networks of both Northern and Southern Ireland. I published my findings, in detail, on the 'Tits' website, but they can be summarised as follows.

Vodka is cheaper in Poland than Ireland. Six barrels of Guinness, divided by 350 people, goes 248 miles. Poland is colder, Ireland is Greener, nobody in Poznan speaks Irish, half of Dublin speak Polish. All railwaymen are the same.

We blasted out of Manchester Victoria one September morning, leaving the old and the new of this great Lancashire city behind us, in a 'Turner' dawn. By eight o'clock we were drumming down the beautiful Lune Gorge at eighty miles an hour, the perfect white exhaust rolling out behind and above us, like a rope cloud. A truly magical moment, that stopped the whole train chattering, and temporarily put the buffet car out of business, as the stewards and waiters, as well as all the passengers, clung to, and hung out of, all the windows, to witness this unique and inspiring spectacle.

In November 2003, Tony Avery and his partner Denise joined us as full members. Tony had a laid-back self-deprecating 'brummie' sense of humour, (God knows he needed it, being a Blues fan), a good voice for singing, and an enduring enthusiasm for early rock n' roll classics. Together with a wide knowledge and love of all things railway, and particularly New Street and London Midland, and a more than passing acquaintance with half the pubs in England, we were bound to get on like a house on fire.

Denise was vivacious, witty, and did a great Celia Johnson impression, as we visited the celebrated Carnforth tea-shop one day, "I think I've got something in my eye." As a woman, she introduced a measure of glamour and decorum into the society, three attributes sadly missing without her.

Richard and I caused an international incident in Carlisle, well actually Richard caused it, pointing out to a Scotsman on a visit across the border, that it was only English money keeping the Celtic nation afloat. 'Will ye no come back again' became not a request, but an order. The haggis basher became quite upset, but we managed to keep just the right side of fisticuffs.

We sang together in Canterbury Cathedral, 'Will no one rid me of this meddlesome cat?', searched in vain for Eric Morecambe's statue in his home town, on a day when the weather was so awful you couldn't see the bay, even from the promenade, and I walked in the sea, fully clothed in Aberystwyth, when it rained so hard the marine walk was the driest part of the visit.

In October Trevor died suddenly, with no history of illness, it came as a terrible shock to us all. Just a couple of weeks before we had all been together on the Severn Valley Railway, and had stayed into the night, talking happily over a couple of drinks. Andy had remarked that I looked tired, and truth to tell, I was not in the best of health. I remember thinking, in fact, how well all the other members of the gang appeared to be.

An autumnal mist hugged the river Severn and the railway, as we click-clacked our way up to Bridgnorth, the red and green signal lights looming up suddenly on their ghostly gantries. Friendly golden yellow gas lamps threw their shadows across the station platforms, and the simmering locomotives hissed and gurgled, their work over for the day, as the night pressed in and drew its veil across the running shed.

Returning home, we finally bid the Severn, now a winding, moonlit, silver stream, a last farewell and toasted each other, and the wonders of steam.

With agreement and approval of the company, we placed a plaque on one of Kidderminster's platform benches, a final reminder of Trev, a kindly, genial friend, and the finest introduction to the railway that so many visitors had ever met.

Some of the impetus had begun to leave the society, and Andy particularly, who had been Trevor's best friend, did ever less tours as the year progressed.

Tony and Denise joined with us, to present the new face of T.I.T.S.

In January of 2006, after a brave battle with cancer, Tony left us. The Christmas train to Chester proved to be his final journey with us. He never grumbled or bemoaned his fate, but his suffering must have been intense. He was a natural, warm and friendly man, much admired and respected by all the travelling railway enthusiasts, and the tour operators and staff.

On a dark and chilly January morning, Past Time Rail's 'Bradford Circular' tour ran with a commemorative wreath upon the locomotive's smokebox. A much appreciated and fitting tribute to Tony.

This really marked the end of the TITS chapter, but when we travel now, we remaining three, and our new colleagues, drink often to absent friends.

As tales of past feats and 'atrocities' are brought to mind, the ghosts are always close at hand, but warm friendly ghosts, and their laughter echoes still, across my mind.

CHAPTER TWENTY SIX

4.10 to Poznan

I looked out through my wing-seat window and watched the little puffs of dust kick up, as the wheels touched down, and we landed gently at Tegel Airport in Berlin. It was the first Sunday in March 2003. The sky was blue, and up above, the moon was new and so was love.

None of that sentence is true; well, none of it after 'March 2003'. It's a verse from Cole Porter's 'Lover Come Back', and it was running through my head, chasing the champagne I had been drinking on the flight. Could you see the new moon in a blue sky, I thought; Cole Porter didn't care, I didn't care, it was a great song, I was not too drunk yet to be romantically and lyrically inquisitive, and I was really excited about the next week or so in Germany and Poland.

The bus into the city took about 40 minutes, it was my first time in Berlin, and all thoughts of contrived lyrics disappeared, as I disembarked at Kurfurstendamm Square, the stop for Bahnhof Zoo. What a great name for a station……. 'Zoo'.

Back home the 'corporate apparatchicks' have been longing to change the name of Birmingham New Street for about 20 years. They keep floating their pitiful substitutes into the public domain, desperately hoping that as the mental capacity of the public continues to degenerate, one of their pathetically banal ideas will catch on.

We've had all the usual, meaningless, 'white hot relevant', bullshit-nonsense, buzz words pressed upon us: 'Central', 'Interchange', 'Metro' etc, under the jargon barrage that the existing name no longer gives out the 'right message' as to the stations 'meaningful function'. For fuck sake, what do they think all those poor lost souls are doing, swarming in and out of this satanic urinal every day; desperately seeking a hymn-book seller, and hoping to form a choir?

Berlin gives us the lead. Let's call it Birmingham Zoo. I accept precedents, I know the city did indeed once have a zoo, sadly now closed, but it was cramped, overcrowded, unhygienic, dirty, uninspiring and totally failed to provide the necessary basic requirements for the comfort and safety of its inhabitants. It was deemed totally unfit for purpose. So there we have it, exactly; 'New Street Zoo' it is.

I was to come back to the square to stay, after my Polish adventure, and as I took my leave of it, the Kaiser Wilhelm Memorial Church became floodlit. It was smashed by the RAF during the latter days of the war, but its spire, although snapped off by bombs, half way to its pinnacle, still thrusts its way skyward. Its lighting only serves to underline its pugnacious determination to break through the enclosing darkness.

It is the most perfect metaphor for human futility and heroic stupidity. We illuminate our graveyards and cenotaphs, but cannot afford a candle to burn a hole in the darkness that leads down all the highways to war and destruction.

I joined the Berlin-Warsaw Express at 6.30pm, and sat back in my comfortable compartment seat, closed the door and began to contemplate the worrying prospect of becoming sober. It was an ill-founded fear; within minutes, a friendly steward came in to see me, and a couple of beers and a ghastly bratwurst ensured the gastric juices weren't crying out for attention.

At Frankfurt on Oder, the train stopped. This was the Germany-Poland border. A coterie of guards, representing both nations, all carrying rifles, entered the compartment. In the dark stillness, it was very John Le Carre. "Passport please." "My mother's goldfish only plays Mozart on the harpsichord." "Ah, but of course, welcome to Poland." They smiled and went about their interrogatory business. I thought to myself, 'good job they didn't know Biffo and I had got the glider hidden in the buffet-car toilet'.

At 9.30pm we arrived at Zbaszynek. I stepped from the train onto the gas-light hissing, mist shrouded, silent, empty platform. The train pulled out and through the swirling, steamy night, four figures materialised. It was like that moment when Roberta finally met her father in the film 'The Railway Children'. Except that she didn't say, "Hey mate, where's the bleedin' taxi to Wolszytyn then?" We all shook hands, exchanged names, bratwurst and beer fumes, and expletives about Polish station names, and headed off down the underpass to the station exit.

I think at this point, it's only fair to mention that there are only nine original letters in the Polish alphabet. As you can see, the above destination has already used up eight of them. I say only fair, because as we progress in this narrative, I may possibly make some up. I think as a rule of thumb, you'll know when I'm doing this, when you don't cover the page with spittle as you attempt the pronunciation.

Within a few minutes of our arrival on the road outside the station, a large black limo drew up and we were vaporised into the night, with not a word spoken, between us five and the anonymous black-clad driver. Although no-one voiced the opinion, I think we were all greatly relieved when we pulled up at the Society house and met by Howard Jones.

Howard and his brother Trevor conceived the 'Wolsztyn Experience', whereby complete novices are allowed to drive steam trains, carrying fare-paying passengers, over a selection of Poland's main line, on scheduled services. No prior driving experience is necessary and no tuition course is given upon arrival. Introduce that concept into your next conversation with an 'Elf and Safety' zealot, and watch the colour drain from his face.

It was after 10.00pm when we arrived at the house, which was not only the 'Experience' head quarters, but also our lodging house for the next week, and Howard doled out the first of many Polish beers from the fridge and gave us a potted history of the genesis and progress made, since he domiciled himself in Wolsztyn, about 10 years earlier. Poland was then, and still is, the only country in Europe, where steam survives on regular main line duty and the steam depot here is also unique on the continent.

Howard told us the Poles had been extremely co-operative, and although they had suffered setbacks, by and large, the enterprise has grown, to the present situation, whereby driving courses operate almost right through the year, and are booked up twelve months in advance.

He related tales of earlier endeavours, some of them amusing, some heart warming, and one or two definitely in the 'I appear to have left my wits, in a state of mind-blowing fear' category. Since his arrival here, Howard has taken up with a local lass, and become fluent in Polish and Terror. With this rich vein of thought-provoking conversation now in full cry, one of our number asked if anyone had been so overcome with the whole experience, that he couldn't manage to drive the loco. 'H' replied that only one guy, in all the ten years had found it all too much for him. Apparently when the Polish crew had managed to prise his bloodless white, straining fingers off the cab door guard rail, they'd thrown him off the footplate and told him to 'Fuck off back to your mother'. In unison, we all drained another beer and decided we'd be better off pissed and compliant, even if scared rigid, than thumbing a lift back to Berlin in the morning.

Thus, full of lager, and heartened by 'H's exhortations, and group-induced bravado, in response to Howard's request, I did what no-one should ever do, in a team-leader, team-player situation...... I volunteered. Not to make the tea, or sleep on the top bunk, but to take the first turn the following day. As the others were paired off together, I would be on my own, with the Polish crew, of course.

It seemed like a good idea at the time. Until I realised the time was 12.00 midnight, and was told my train would be the 4.10am off Wolsztyn, to Poznan. I was given a set of directions, and was told the station was about 20 minutes walk from the house. Christ, I thought, it'll take me twenty minutes to get up the stairs.

I sat on my bed in the cold dark confines of my room. In about 3-1/2 hours I would be driving a fully loaded passenger train to Poland's second city. My mental state was swinging, pendulum-like, between apprehensive and terrified, with a little numbness thrown in for ballast. I'd been 'steam barmy' all my life, but my driving experience to date could be logged on a matchbox label; in fact it could be engraved on a match, on one side. I'd taken two driving stints, on the Great Central Railway, on Gala days. Total mileage covered, about two, duration, about ten minutes, top speed, 25 mph.

I looked through bloodshot eyes at our time-table for the morrow's trip. 81 kilometers, 16 station stops, scheduled running time, 2 hours 4 minutes. Piece of piss, I thought, and fell into a comatose replica of sleep, clutching my alarm clock to my bosom. I kept on all my travelling clothes, except my shoes. My eyelids had just met in closure, when the alarm went off. I started up in bed, banged my head on the headboard lamp, fell out of the cot, tripped over my discarded shoes, and scraped my shins on the cleverly positioned bedside cabinet.

I heard Howard outside say "You ok Bruce?", I mumbled an affirmative and began to dress for the coming exertions. Off with trousers, on with thick overalls, off with chic, 'city gent' travelling shirt, on with coarse Polish check version. On with thermal socks, hard toe-cap boots. Finally, drivers coat, short scarf and woolly hat. Grabbing my lunch-bag, I plunged through the darkness, surf-boarded down the stairs, and after several abortive attempts, located my key in the door-lock. I fell out into the Polish pre-dawn morning. Fucking Hell! It was freezing, minus 18 degrees I was told later.

My breath came out in a solid blast and fell to the ground, my eyebrows frosted up, and the liquid in my nose froze inside my nostrils as I sniffed. Ice was packed solid on the road and footpath, and an ingot of ice ran the whole length of the gutter. The road shone with silvery diamonds beneath the yellow street lights.

I strode off purposefully down the road to the station, where a silver-white plume of smoke rose vertically on the horizon: The boys were ready for me, and I was ready for them.

I crunched along the platform, through the freezing and frozen snow, sliding in and out of the footprints of earlier walkers, (who in heaven's name could they have been?), until I reached my steam-hissing, headlight-glowing, black, shining, snow-flecked steel, wonder horse of PKP: Polish Railways. She was a class Ol49, number 69, of 2-6-2 wheel arrangement, weighing 120 tonnes. Because of Europe's larger loading gauge than ours, she was massively proportioned, and I could discern enough room on her footplate, between engine and tender, to hold a barn-dance. To say I was impressed was a huge under-statement. Her side-doors were shut tight, and the canopy was drawn down across the cab and tender roof, whilst a rose-red glow danced and flickered inside the window panes. Outside, where I stood, it was cold enough to freeze Brandy. It was an awe-inspiring moment.

I rapped tentatively on the cab door, and eventually, silently, it swung open. Grasping the hand rails firmly, I gingerly ascended the steps to the footplate. I hauled myself inside, leaving the skin off the palms of both my hands, on the metal. In my haste to leave the boarding house, I'd forgotten my gloves. The temperature reminded me of this oversight; I wouldn't do it again.

My driver was Henryk, who turned out to be a man of few words; only one, in fact, although he did repeat it thirty two times, 'Odjazd', which for two days I thought meant 'eff off', but in fact turned out to be the more politically correct 'depart'.

As we waited for the 'off', he sat me on the driver's seat, on the right hand side of the cab, like our Western Region engines, and gave me my driving induction course. He acquainted me with the regulator, and with the help of the firemen's more fluent (several words!) conversation, made sure I didn't cross the 1.0 mark on the gauge when I opened up at departure time. The reverser was 'marked' from 60% to 30%, which is how I drove the engine, in three cut-off movements, and the brake, which I used through 'apply', 'lap', and back to 'drive' as we eased, hopefully, to a successful halt in the station. Finally I was shown the whistle, which was to be in almost constant use on this run, and that was that. It all took about two minutes. So; I was a driver.

Henryk looked at the station clock, the engine 'brewed up', the fireman opened the fire-doors and began to fill the grate, the guard whistled, Henryk shouted 'Odjazd', tapped my shoulder and stepped back behind me. I pushed up the regulator, watched the 1.0 mark on the glass, and Glory, Glory, the bloody train started to 'bark' her way out of Wolsztyn station. I looked back through the cab window, and realised, for the first time, that I had on, three 'double-decker' passenger coaches. They were full of people. I was driving them. They didn't know. I was almost hysterical. But in an inward, bursting, very English way. What a fantastic, sensational, feeling.

The next 124 minutes were the most exhilarating of my life. In order to maintain the most exacting schedule, which was the same as that allotted to diesel traction, we blasted out of every station, and racing through the cut off positions whilst pushing the regulator ever higher, we were running up to fifty miles an hour within about three minutes of departure. With the maximum distance between the stops no more than 8 kilometres, it was then time to begin to ease-down the regulator, and wind back the screw. Then, "close regulator", and the most demanding part of the drive, stopping the train within the platform length.

In the pitch dark, with the stations unlit, platforms only about 2 feet high, and all the stops seemingly in heavily forested areas, this was only achieved due to the Polish crew's wonderful and comprehensive knowledge of 'the road'.

As we sat in the silent, empty stations, our engine hissing and fussing, without announcement, people began to appear, like ghosts, from the embrace of the brooding, eternal forest. As they approached the train, the sliding doors of the compartments opened, and they disappeared into the yellow beam of friendly light, like aliens returning to their space-ship. Then 'Odjazd', yet again, and off we tore, into the burgeoning light of the icy, smoke-breathing dawn.

The stops came and went as in a dream. We thrashed across countless level crossings, whistling frantically, as traffic waited, even in these very early hours, at all of them. Fifteen intermediate stations, and I couldn't spell, nor pronounce, any of them. Me, the master of English and Geography; but this was Polish and Gibberish. What a very singular nation this is, when every city and township is named using only those nine base letters. And specially since three of them are W, Y and Z.

In what seemed no time at all, a pall of smoke and a whiff of sulphur, hanging on the lightening dawn, announced our arrival in the suburbs of Poznan. Henryk took over the 'seat', as we forged through vast carriage sidings and marshalling yards. No signal could be overlooked in this mightily complex, congested, chaotic spiders web. Trains were passing us on either side; suburban stock, single and double-deckers, Warsaw – Berlin expresses, lumbering freight trains, empty-stock shunters. Miraculously we rolled into our allotted platform, in the city's impressive station, and our 'cargo' disembarked, away to the mills and factories to earn their living, on yet another day, to return later on a dark evening train, to their hidden forest homes.

The morning light had now come up and I sat, as railwaymen do, my elbow at the window's sill, my PKP driver's hat set back, at a jaunty angle, on my head, and affected that nonchalant demeanour, as one does, after a boring job, effortlessly done. In reality, my vitals were ablaze, my emotions cascading into each other, and adrenalin was dripping from my ears. My 'public image' and the real me, were as far divorced from one another as a politician and the truth, and nearly as antithetical as Satan and Cliff Richard. A good trick if you can pull it off.

We had arrived at 6.20am, right on time. I managed to keep myself just the right side of hyper-ventilation, and was drifting down into that glorious feeling of peace within, and peace within the world. I was also beginning to feel decidedly hungry, in a state, I suppose, of grace and flavour.

Both the Polish boys and I had brought our lunch bags with us, the difference being that theirs contained sandwiches and fruit, and mine held a couple of pairs of thermal socks and a map of the London Underground. With a nod to Henryk, who tapped his watch knowingly, I climbed off the footplate and went in search of breakfast.

With the gift, or is it the curse, that has either dogged or led me, all my life, into ludicrous unconventionality, I found myself in the only spaghetti restaurant in Poznan; perhaps in Poland. Certainly the only one open, and buzzing with life at 6.30 in the morning. I ordered a Bolognese. I wolfed it down as if it were my last meal. It tasted so much better than socks or the Underground map. The coffee was hot, full-bodied and invigorating. As I stood, waiting to pay, I caught sight of myself in the mirror behind the counter. Well, I caught sight of a creature, face streaked with oil and coal-dust, hair dark and lank, journeying in many directions; jacket scorched and overalls burnt around the turnups, and a filthy scarf most unlike a lady's favour, sweat-soaked and clinging to its throat. No one in the thronging little bistro took a blind bit of notice. "Christ!" I thought, "I'm a real bloody railwayman". I had a spring in my step, as I made my way back to the station; I looked like Al Jolson, and began to sing to myself in the manner of that precursor of the musical movie genre;

"I'd walk a million miles,

To kiss Nobby Stiles......"

Henryk was busy with the oil-can, checking all the lubrication points on number 69's motion, shining and steel glinting, as it caught the first light of a watery sun.

The fireman was busy building up the fire, expertly placing his shovelful's of Katowice coal, making sure he had an even cover all across the grate, and a strong black exhaust towered into the morning sky, announcing our imminent departure. 8.10am, a long pull on the whistle and away we went through the metal maze, on our way back to Wolsztyn. Again there were thunderous departures, strident whistling, hair-raising halts, but now, with a clear blue sky and the scent of pine-needles in my nostrils, I was beginning to enjoy the experience, as my awareness, and confidence grew.

No longer straining my eyes to see signals, whistle-board warnings, and approaching level-crossings, I was able to look around me, and take in the passing panorama. Above us, buzzards soared in their thermal climbs; wings wide and fingertip stretched, with just the occasional lazy beat, to push them ever higher in the unseen vortex of their heavenly delight. Peregrines raced from the seclusion of the forest, to snatch their songbird prey, and disappear once more into the conifer gloom. Families of deer dashed suddenly from the woods, crossing the tracks only yards ahead of us; a pair of wild boar were busy snuffling and truffling in the frosty undergrowth, and gave us barely the time of day. Now, in the daylight, the station buildings were visible, built in a strange architectural fusion of Dutch gable and Norwegian chalet. Around each stopping place, a few small houses huddled, and then the whole, vast open plain stretched away for as far as the eye could see, broken with huge forested areas, but flat, with no high ground apparent.

As we raced across the country, I couldn't help thinking of September 1939, when two new words were heard in Europe for the first time, words that were to reverberate across the whole world, and bring nightmarish terror to countless millions. 'Blitz krieg'; lightning war, Hitler's army, led by divisions of light, speedy, but heavily armoured fast-firing tanks, followed by a highly mobile infantry, and supported from above by the hordes of screaming Stuka dive-bombers, were unleashed upon an unsuspecting and totally unprepared Poland. They were met not far from the Capital, Warsaw, by the Polish cavalry regiments. Men burnished swords and stirrups, polished leather boots and saddles, and groomed their wonderful martial horses. One can only half imagine the horror, and shock, which their riders were to experience, as the apocalypse bore down upon them, in what was to be the last cavalry engagement in twentieth century history. It was over in minutes, the field strewn with the dead and dying, men and their mounts, and only the ghastly trinket hunters moving amongst the carnage. Only ghouls and horses.

These fields and forests are quieter now, but the memory of that fearful day, and the countless other days of cruel subjugation that followed, are etched deep into the Polish psyche.

"O what can ail thee, wretched wight,
Alone and palely loitering?

The sedge has withered from the lake,
And no birds sing."

As these images faded from my mind, all too soon, the Leszno line trailed in to meet us, and we began the approach to Wolsztyn.

On my final day with Henryk, he would let me bring the train into the station, a highly pleasing confirmation of his confidence in my ability; but not this first time. I stepped back behind him, as he took over the drivers' seat, and felt, even in the still, freezing air of the mid-morning, a growing warmth of inner satisfaction. It was the first experience of a wondrous week, of gracious, friendly, hard working engine-men, dedicated to the cause of the steam locomotive, golden lager beer, lip-burning vodka, and pretty barmaids.

Of powerful, inspiring locomotives, skin-chafing, muscle aching 'disposal' duties on the shed, water turning to ice in your hair, as the 'bag' overflowed, coal dust in your ears, your eyes, and halfway up your nose, as the coal-plant escalator emptied its buckets into the ever-hungry tender; bloody knuckles and scraped knees as you slammed the levers to and fro to clean the grate fire-bars. Clothes like a ragamuffin, face like a demon, breath straight from Satan's bottom.

Oh, the pure, glorious, filthy, painful, wonderful, fucking joy of it all.

I have my 'facsimile' number plate of Ol49-69, my few poor photographs, and my vivid memories, that will last as long as I do.

I am proud to have worked with the railwaymen of Wolsztyn, and glad to have been part of this little miracle, even for but one short moment of time.

Wolszytn's finest. Europe's last main-line steam drivers

CHAPTER TWENTY SEVEN

Thoughts and Pictures on a Train Through France

Sunday

From Worcester's Foregate Street to the Llanguedoc,
'Mind the Gap' to Carcassonne,
Banks' beer to Roussillon,
Inter City 125 to Grand Vitesse:
What a culture shock.
First Class Eurostar from Waterloo,
Battersea Power Station and Wandsworth Road,
Wining and Dining, nothing else to do.
The romance of the Golfe de Lion
Is a million light years distant,
From this drab, grey, abode.
Folkestone's old lady, hands on her hips,
We're under her skirts and the Channel's Ships,
Forty two minutes in the tunnel of love:
Then the Somme, Pas De Calais, time to get to grips
With men and rifles, no songbirds or sparrows.
Harry Monmouth was here too,
French nobles felled by bows and arrows.
The tingling sadness of northern France,
Where death played the fiddle
At the Kaiser's dance.
White painted mileposts, white marble graves,
English, Canadian, Australian braves;
Lovingly remembered in farmers fields
Not by European slaves.
Through Ile De France we begin to slow,
As fields disappear, the tenements grow.
Modesty, decorum, both fall on their swords,
Stade de France, Sacre Coeur, Gare de Nord;
The World cup, God, and a railway station,

Welcome to the heart of a civilised nation.
Before we leave her and head off South,
Paris kisses you full on the mouth.
Palm fringed platforms at the Gare de Lyon,
Double-decker train, upstairs, soon zooming
On a gourmet journey of cities, looming;
Brie, Beaune, Dijon, Macon, Beajolais,
I'm travelling through a menu at 'grande vitesse',
This is French fast food, without the stress.
The Rhone Valley darkens, but the train's not slowing,
Snow capped Alps in the half light, glowing.
We glide to a halt in a bouquet of drizzle,
And catch the aroma of a pork chop sizzle;
I joyously splash in the rain of Provence.
No boisterous, roisterous, big city noise; quiet Avignon sighs.

Monday

The morning brings the Mistral's blow,
Sand-dried, the signal for the rains to go.
Steam rises from the medieval, marble streets,
Inquisition horror stories, Templar defeats,
To the great gothic palace, full of dead French Popes,
On to Benezet's bridge, built on dreams and hopes,
But only halfway over the river to Arles.
'Sur le Pont D'Avignon, L'on y danse, tout en ronde'.
Passing Nimes, Montpelier, Beziers, Narbonne,
All thoughts of the northern Capital gone.
This French linguistic, 'West country' loner,
Is nearer to Gloucester and Barcelona.
The tricolour is almost dead;
Here the colours are yellow and red.
Flamingo's wade in an inland sea,
Buzzards are wheeling in a Van Gogh sky,
The Mediterranean is close by.
Perpignan, 'Centre of the World',

So Salvador Dali named its railway station.
Leaving the nightmare of Franco's Spain,
To find his Catalan liberation.
Wide boulevards roll down to Horloge Square,
Then cobbled streets, with chattering cafes,
Red-brick churches, accordions playing;
Steel hawsers hold the Palm trees down,
Already they are full date-laden,
Lizards are sunbathing everywhere.
Black and white striped people sit under
Green umbrellas,
The dry, warm wind breathes a sweet aroma,
Paella, prawns frying, olives and pasta,
Herbs and spices, senses in a coma.
I spend all night in the 'Casa Sansa';
A Pay D'oc restaurant extravaganza.
All around the room swim the menu fish,
Aquaria lit with green light glow.
We wink at each other as they pass me by
We're already friends, I have to let them know.
Soup, escargots, beef and rice; deep Grenach Noir wine
And Cognac flow.
I talk with Belgians, church bells chime:
We all hear midnight come and go.

Tuesday

'The Hotel Paris and Barcelona';
Commerce must tip its cap both ways in this
Part of France,
Wall-painted rally cries, 'Catalan Libre', 'Catalan Sempre',
As yet the rebellion keeps an even temper:
But soon it won't be such a merry dance.
I climb aboard the little yellow train, 'Le petite traine
Jeune' of Pyrennes fame;
Ahead, the smouldering mountains stretch away to Spain

Under hissing wires we rattle and shake
Into the green bowl of the Canigou,
Smoke and steam rising all around,
Above us buzzards soar, there is no sound;
We're in a cauldron of mountain stew,
A silent, Franco-Iberian ragout.
Thanks to the crew, a taxi stands in the bay,
Spain is just a signal-box away.
The village is a quiet, secret, hill retreat,
Time for a la carte lunch at five thousand feet.
A medieval Manor, in a sleepy-dog street,
Basking in sunshine between sun flowers
They dream their bone-filled dreams for hours.
To pass through the door, I bend my head,
In this timber-framed wonder,
In this timeless spot:
A vast dining hall is set out before me,
I'm in the banquet room of Camelot.
Tables and seating, enough for hundreds,
The waiter in black, arrives silently,
I'm joined by a dog and the village priest.
He reads his bible and clasps his hands,
I'm in the refectory that time forgot.
This is my finest meal in all of France:
My table is set for a gathering of gourmets.
Dining alone, but with food enough for twenty,
One whole ham, blushing and moist,
A huge spicy sausage, a plate of feather sliced meat
Off the bone.
A jar of fat young gherkins,
Chives and capers in an olive oil drizzle;
Slabs of roast beef to build your house with,
Warm and wonderful, aromatic bread.
Rock salt, black pepper corns and thick French mustard,
And a plate to sail home in.
A square, litre bottle of blood-red, almost black, thick,

Vein-surging, cheek warming Roussillon:
A local cognac, fiery and fortifying, harsh strong black coffee.
I've ordered everything in bruised French.
I rise to leave and wish the couple who have
Surreptitiously joined me, a gentle good day and goodbye.
They return the compliments in a rich Lancashire accent;
They're on holiday from Blackburn.
The little yellow train is waiting for me.
The driver invites me into the cab for the
Helter-skelter journey back down the mountain.
A look at his watch, then he steps from the train,
And at the platform's end, pisses gently into
The close, green couch grass.
We rush, dizzily down the twisting turning line.
A cigarette dangles from his lips; window open,
The smoke mingles with the cooling, misting air
Of the enclosing evening.
Shadows lengthen, we're descending steeper, faster,
Darker into hell.
The yellow-light twinkling town comes into view:
No cloven hooves for a day or two.
I am completely happy.

Wednesday

A leisurely stroll into palm tree square,
Menthol cigarette smoke in the dust blown air;
'La Monde', a croissant, two strong Irish coffees,
Gallic breakfast chic is everywhere.
A final circuit of the old town centre,
A goodbye Ricard, and some lizard spotting,
The TGV for some high speed trotting,
Back along the fringe of the lazy lapping 'Med',
Under the shadow of the Cevennes.
To Lyons, the Cote de Rhone, St. Etienne,
The Gare de Lyon, Paris early evening glow;

The city's buzzing for the Motor Show.
'Hotel Lux', not the best I've ever seen,
But the insects are friendly and the bedroom's clean.
Out on metro 5, (Pablo Picasso),
I decide to dine in La Place Bastille.
Many French aristos' did, for their last evening meal.
A column marks the site of the revolution prison,
A golden statue towers over dark oblivion,
Parisiens roar round this great traffic wheel,
Once again the people are imprisoned in steel.
The Eiffel tower is visible at the head of the Champs,
There are stars in the sky, music tumbles from L'Opera,
The grand lady is vibrant, and wears her Beouf
Bourguignon perfume, just a touch recklessly at her
Breast, I am seduced yet again by her.
'Chez Paul' in the Rue de Charonne, A theatrical
Bolt-hole, throngs with exotic, beautiful and not so
Beautiful people. The Great are not always good.
The chef is cutting up his beef steaks;
Other meat was cut here before.
Another bottle of Cote's de Rhone, comes out with me,
Into the heady Paris evening.
A final Ricard at a pavement Café, and I drift
Dreamily back to my insect time-share.

Thursday

The Gare du Nord is a massive, mighty monument
To French industrial greatness.
Inter City Expresses roll in and out, to Belgium
Holland, Germany, Luxembourg and Britain.
Truly, the 'Ice Train' cometh.
The human wretchedness of the city sleep on the
Floor at the portals of this transport shrine.
The poor are always without tickets.
'Eurostar' snakes out into the flats and apartments of La Chapelle.

We dive under the elevated runway of France's
Premier airport. As ever, Charles De Gaulle, is above
All others in France.
Time passes; at 185 miles per hour, very quickly.
I wake up in the county of Kent,
It's "afternoon mate", "Bonjour" is spent.
Into Waterloo's 'spiders web', a brand new station,
Soon to be redundant;
Replaced by a Victorian configuration,
St. Pancras will then be our destination.
Now I'm old and weary, through and through,
But Paris and France will keep me new.
Back to the city in 'Printemps', perchance,
Reborn in a gallic renaissance.

CHAPTER TWENTY EIGHT

Curry Brendaloo
(Very Hot & Spicy)

INGREDIENTS

60ml Ghee. 1 large onion. 6 dried red chillies. 3 cloves. 10ml cumin. 10ml coriander. 10ml paprika. 10 black peppercorns. 10ml mustard seeds. 10 garlic cloves. 90ml white vinegar. 900gms pork shoulder. 4 litres Carlsberg lager. 750cl Pinot Noir Burgundy. 6 measures Vodka. 4 Angostura bitters. 400ml vomit.

PREPARATION

1. Heat half the Ghee in a heavy pan. Add onion and fry over a moderate heat. Drink 1 litre Carlsberg, 1 measure Vodka.
2. Remove onion from the casserole and place in blender. Drink ½ litre Carlsberg, 1 measure Vodka.
3. Add chillies, spices, garlic, salt and vinegar, then 60mg water. Work until completely smooth. Drink 1 litre Carlsberg, 1 measure Vodka.
4. Cut the pork into 2.5ml cubes, heat remainder of ghee in the pan, add pork and fry over a moderate heat. Add onions and spice mixture, cook over high heat, constantly stirring. Drink 1 litre Carlsberg, 1 measure Vodka.
5. Turn heat down low, cover and cook for about 1-1/2 hours. Drink 750cl Pinot Noir Burgundy, 1 measure Vodka.

SERVING SUGGESTION FOR ALFRESCO DINING

Present onto warmed plate with plain boiled rice, raita and mango chutney. Find suitable flat-topped wall approx 2 ft high. Sit on wall with plate held close to stomach, then gently fall backwards.
Pull the plate up and down your body, ensuring an even spread of

curry covers all your clothing.
Roll over on the ground. Whilst face down, introduce vomit (400ml) into the mix.
Roll over again.
Don't forger to work the curry into your hair with your fingers.
Now fall asleep for approx. 2-1/2 hours.

FINISHING OFF

On awakening, drink the remaining ½ litre of Carlsberg, and the last measure of Vodka.
Rinse your hair in the angostura bitters.
If you have not broken your mobile phone whilst rolling about on the floor, call the ambulance. Give them your blood group, allergy information, liver donor card number, and next of kin details.
Bon appetite!
Recipe from "Have fun with food", by Brenda McKay. (Hodder Press 220p £12.99).

CHAPTER TWENTY NINE

Tapestry

The Alps by night, through the windows of a plane,
Sitting on a Goa beach, in warm, pouring rain.
A Hampshire stream brimmed with watercress,
William A. Stanier F.R.S.
Dylan Thomas, John Milton, Robert Frost;
The Road less travelled, Paradise Lost?
Thomas Hardy, Shelley, Jack Kerouac
On the Road, with Salinger's knapsack
On his back.

Gedda, Callas, Bjoerling, Domingo,
Kenya's Navasha Lake,
The flight of a Flamingo.
Caravaggio's 'Supper' and 'Cupid Sleeping',
Pitlochry's water ladder, silver salmon leaping.
JMW Turner and 'The Fighting Temeraire',
Rembrandt, Rodin, 'The White Polar Bear';
Musee D'Orsay, What a Paris revelation,
Van Gogh, Monet, Seurat in a railway station.

Steam and Bathams glorious beer
On the Severn Valley,
Ben Webster's 'Honeysuckle Rose', an A4 on the 'Tally'.
Frank Sinatra, Sammy Davis, cool Dean Martin,
The Ratpack with neat haircuts and a left side parting.
Mist over Shap Fell, a new day dawning,
Childhood innocence on Christmas morning.
Alf Ramsey, Alan Ball, noble Bobby Moore,
The dream, and the twin towers, broken on the floor.

Jazz on the Left Bank, and 'Roger the Frog',
All the things in William Shatner's Captain's Log.

The Prix de L'Arc de Triomphe
Masquerading as 'Le punter',
The Beano, Wizard, Hotspur and Billy Bunter.
Ghento, Puskas, De Stefano, Real Madrid
Cruyff, George Best, Pele, all that Brazil did.
Rocky Marciano and Sylvester the Cat,
Jack in the 'Cuckoo's Nest',
James Stewart, "I'm aware of that".

Marilyn Monroe, Kim Novak, James Dean,
Muhammed Ali, 'Mad' magazine.
Sammy Turner's 'Always', Garbo so aloof,
Winter lights twinkling under Paddington's roof.
Bobby Darin, Nat King Cole and Peggy Lee;
Jesse Norman, Kathleen Battle, Rosa Ponselle,
'Rigoletto', 'Don Giovanni' dropping down to hell.
Norwegian waterfalls in late spring flood,
Richard Burton's opening words in 'Under Milk Wood'.

'Johnno', 'Wilko', 'Billy Whizz', in their tight fitting cossies,
Our World Cup in the Telstra, full of very quiet Aussies.
Barry John, David Duckham, Willie John McBride,
'Merve the swerve' and Gareth Edwards, what a 99 side.
The Empire State, the Chrysler, a Manhattan day breaking,
Steaming manhole covers, and the Subway shaking.
Across the world in Agra
On a dusty night in June,
The Taj Mahal is floating under India's moon.

Lady Day, Sarah Vaughan, Ella clouds my eye,
Every time I hear 'Every time we say goodbye'.
Large regal Elgar's Enigma Variations,
Bix and Louis Armstrong's mystic syncopations.
Irving Berlin, Cole Porter 'Dancing in the dark',
All those friendly duo's in Noah's timely Ark.
Grand Central Station's Oyster Bar, and the Bronx zoo,

A Joey in the pouch of a kangaroo.

Mad Max Wall, silly walk, manic flight,
(A cough), "I must get a room tonight".
Eric Morecambe putting 'Mr Preview' through his paces,
Playing all the right notes, in the wrong places.
Peter Sellers, the Goon Show, Gaping Gill,
Spike Milligan's tombstone told us he was ill.
'Messiah' echoing round Tewkesbury Abbey,
Worcester mothers calling their children 'babby'.
The 'uni-dexter' Mr. Spigot, A.L. Wisty,
Pete and Dud, and Johnny Mathis singing 'Misty'.

Manzi's Restaurant in Leicester Square,
London's finest lobsters and Italian care.
The Palladium, E.N.O., the pubs of Covent Garden,
From street theatre to the bard of Arden.
Elvis, Buddy Holly, Little Richard, Jerry Lee,
Johnny Hodges magic, playing 'All of Me'.
Duke Ellingtons ghost still loves us madly,
Les Dawson's playing Chopin, but very badly.

Coltrane, Gillespie, 'Bird' and Miles,
Charles Dickens, Denis Wheatley and the Ipcress Files.
The MJQ, Dave Brubeck, furious fingered Oscar P,
The Anchor at Cockwood, and a Devon Cream tea.
Dawlish, the sea wall, red sand and blue sea,
'Bill and Ben', 'Mr. Turnip', on black and white TV.
The atomic Count Basie, 'Dock Green's lamp,
'Journey into Space', the lady is a tramp.
Mozart, Shakespeare, the casting of the runes,
Several pints, or maybe more, with the 'Pres' in Wetherspoons.

Strange, how tears in sadness sigh,
But cannot be recalled, without equal thoughts of joy.
Life's a cloth of memories, woven through a throng,

There are times the needles knit with skill,
And times they get the pattern wrong.
It's a melody of fabric, that lasts until you're gone,
One moment you're the singer; Now you are the song.
The people that have loved you,
And those that love you now,
Will lift the spirit, make you smile, when you don't know how.
Warm within this blanket
Through the needle's eye I see,
My friends, the coloured stitches, that are this tapestry.

CHAPTER THIRTY

Craven Images

The omens had been good.

I'd begun a week's holiday in the Yorkshire Dales, talking with a lady called Wensley, who kept a diary. "Mrs. Wensley's Dales Diary", I murmured to myself, "they could make a radio serial out of that." The idea appealed to me, but something nagged away in the half-empty box-rooms in the back of my brain, telling me it had all been done before.

I digress, but then, in my current state, at my advanced time of life, God knows; it's the only thing I'm really good at.

We were sitting, chatting in the lounge of the 'Woolly Sheep' in Skipton, my booked hotel for the weekend. I was drinking Timothy Taylor's best bitter, which I always find a great aid to digression, and she was hoping I would be interesting enough to merit inclusion in her journal.

I'm sure I impressed her: "Sunday; met a man who talked disjointed drivel, and drank rather a lot. Moved on to Grassington."

I'd spent both weekend days storming up to Carlisle and back, on the Settle and Carlisle Railway, 'window hanging' behind my beloved steam traction. Apart from the temporary blindness in my left eye, caused by flying hot embers from the exhaust, and my hair catching fire, as we entered Blea Moor tunnel, the experiences had been exhilarating and fulfilling.

I had marvelled, as I always did, at the unique landscape, as we thundered up to Aisgill, below the brooding majesty of Ingleborough, Whernside and Pen Yghent. Now with my sight, but sadly not all my hair restored, and my bedroom washbasin clogged with spent coal cinders, it was time for me too, to move on, to Clapham in Ribblesdale.

My reasons were twofold:

1) To avoid the wrath of the 'Woolly Sheep' management, when the entire first-floor plumbing system ceased to function, due to carbon infiltration, and
2) To prepare myself mentally and physically, for my forthcoming 'Holiday Challenge', the descent of a huge pit in the earth called Gaping Gill.

I think it only fair to admit at this point, that this diversion had not been my own idea. The credit, or should it be blame, is due entirely to an engaging duo, who, as I have fortunately survived the subterranean ordeal, I can still claim as dear friends, John and Dee, from Solihull.

These two wonderful people rattle round the world, armed only with spam sandwiches and a compass, storming up mountains, plunging down mine-shafts, dragging narrow boats up lock flights, train riding through canyons, and throbbing down highways on motor-bikes, and yes, they come from Solihull.....

Thus it was that under a cloud-scudding, azure sky, on a late August afternoon, I stepped out of a mini-bus from Settle and nimbly into the 'New Inn' at Clapham. It was time to relax, collect my thoughts, plan my strategy, take my valium and sample several pints of Masham's finest, 'Black Sheep'.

It occurred to me that an ovine pattern was beginning to emerge.

The 'New Inn' was the ideal place to begin the adventure. Occupying every available space on every wall, were sepia pictures of men wearing plus-fours, woolly hats and ropes. Captions below told the epic tales of their daring-do, exceptional people all, and left me in no doubt, that strong drink and a sort of madness had been bedfellows for many years in these parts.

Awe-inspiring lithographs of bold northern men-folk, posing nonchalantly, whilst standing on a six-inch ledge of rock deep inside the abyss of the Gill, still devising methods of continuing downwards, even when their plumb lines indicated that the next stop was probably to have horns and a tail fitted, and to choose the exact shade of red, one fancied spending eternity decked out in.

What drove them ever on in this great endeavour, was the fact that a continental caver, from La France, no less, had managed to become the first to plant the tricolour in the mud at the bottom of the pit.

For the rest of the world to accept that Johnny Frenchman was braver and barmier than good Yorkshire folk, could not be tolerated; honour had to be, and of course, was, satisfied.

The afternoon drifted into evening. Battalions of people in big boots and multi-coloured coats, came and went. I ate a fine rack of lamb, then tiredness and the flock of Black Sheep I'd drunk, finally consumed me, thus cleverly getting their own back. An early start beckoned, I gesticulated back, but it took no notice. In a deep sleep, I dreamt of mountains and large holes in the ground. Forsaking breakfast, I strode out of the 'New Inn' at 6.30am. It was already pleasantly warm and the sky was perfectly clear. I stood and listened as the stream chuckled with the stones in its bed, as it danced under the road-bridge in the village centre.

For a few moments I was thrown off my guard, what was that sound? Lord, it was blissful, all encompassing, gloriously invasive, silence.

Desperately trying to recall the directions given to me last night in the pub, I began the ascent of Ingleborough. I couldn't go wrong; it was the very big hill blocking out the light at the end of the village. I had lost my way twice; in the car-park and St. James' churchyard, before, mercifully, a Clapham early riser, on his morning constitutional, put me on the right path.

The first ghost of a misgiving flitted through my mind; I locked it in the 'not to be used again' corner of the brain, and began to climb.

Passing through a clump of ancient, overhanging trees, their trunks clothed in emerald green lichen, a buzzard launched himself lazily from a branch, no more than two feet above me, and I felt the draught from his slow wing-beats, as he swept above my head, almost parting my hair with his nonchalant, dangling legs.

A quiet lake, its surface shimmering glass, appeared between the trees, mallards broke from their reedy cover and forged silently, in vee formation towards the safety of the middle water. I stood for a moment transfixed, in a dreamlike, transcendental state; a painted character in a Millais landscape. The Clapham stream now gurgled its way alongside the footpath, alive with Dipper's, the 'water blackbirds', nodding and bowing like head waiters, in their fine black suits and pristine white waistcoats.

Ingleborough Cave was passed and the real climb to the Gill began.

After leaving the pub and during the entire ascent, save my friendly guide in Clapham, I didn't see another soul.

My legs and lungs were handling the day well, but my feet were beginning to rebel against the borrowed walking boots; however the walk was going well, and I was making civil conversation with the passing sheep. But then a cruel trick. The path disappeared and about two million tons of huge, sharp, unforgiving boulders barred my way, as they cascaded down in an almost vertical defile.

It was at this point, with the blister count rising, and a fear that I had really lost my way, that I almost contemplated turning back. But then, one of my black faced friends, grinning as he clambered past me, picked his way up the fiendish incline and squeezed through the gap at the top. I might fail in this endeavour, I thought, but I'm not going to be outdone by a bloody lamb chop.

Twenty minutes later, bloodied and aching all over, I followed the sheep out of the ravine. I was reminded of an old friends' favourite dictum, "If you can't take a joke, you shouldn't of joined." After negotiating this hazard, a path of sorts became discernible, but then petered out, and only miles of untrodden, windblown, waving grassy slopes stretched out ahead of me, as far as the eye could see.

I forged onwards, but the seed of doubt was growing. Visions of stumbling around in this massive landscape, no maps, no compass, no sense. Then I saw it; a sign propped at an angle beside a tufted hillock; "Gaping Gill ¼ mile." I could have been no more surprised, or delighted, had it been a Wetherspoon's Pub. I was revitalised. Now with a spring, three broken blisters, and half a pint of blood, in my step, like JFK, I "proceeded with vigour".

The great peak of Ingleborough now came into view, and the blustery zephyrs put on their coarser gloves, and slapped, not caressed my face. Water welled up and drove across my eyes, I had difficulty seeing clearly as I breasted the final ridge, then …….. magic!

A straggling, disparate, tented encampment was spread out before me, reaching to the high horizon. Canvas slapped, pennants flapped in the swirling devils of the wind. Guy ropes creaked and sighed, smoke wisps rose and circled in the air. Lowry matchstick figures ducked and weaved between the marquee's with clanking metal pots and pans.

I waited to hear a trumpet fanfare; it was Henry V's final morning before Agincourt. The red on white, and Union flags were flying, "Cry God for Harry, England and St. George." I pressed on, until I came at last to the very edge of the crater, the huge indentation in the ground, covering a vast area. It was a truly awesome sight and the winch platform and surrounding equipment stores were dwarfed in comparison.

It was a timeless, haunting place, and as I cupped my hands over my eyes to turn and survey the further limits of the excavation, I caught my breath in amazement. There, on a stark, high outcrop of rock, was a brown beige dog, perfectly still, save for his large ears flapping in the driving wind.

He sat on his haunches, completely without fear, and as my vision cleared for just a second, I realised this wondrous animal, oblivious to the savage beauty of his surroundings, was pissing, long and heavily, into Gaping Gill. Through rheumy eyes I marvelled at his bravery, his composure, and yes, his mightily enduring stamina. On and on, impossibly, his relief continued; what in God's name had he been drinking last night?

The wind suddenly abated, my eyes began to clear, it finally dawned upon me at last; he wasn't real, but a facsimile, a stuffed canine, complete with running hosepipe, hidden between his paws.

The talisman of the Craven Pothole Club; what a fine ambassador, what a stunning introduction.

I began to think already of my new acquaintances, as Margaret Thatcher (almost) said of Gorbachev: "These are people I can do business with."

I walked down to the tent nearest to the winch mechanism and was greeted by the ladies and gentlemen of the club, who were about to open up the 'shop' for business.

It was just on 8.30am. I was the only customer. They all agreed that as I was there, they may as well get the show on the road, or under the road, I suppose. In exchange for ten pounds I was given a helmet and a brass numbered disc to wear around my neck. To identify the body later, I assumed. I turned it over, expecting it to be engraved, "I promise to pay the Craven Club £10 to be lowered at frightening speed, through a deluge of freezing water, into the impenetrable darkness of a bottomless pit." It didn't, but that was pretty close to what actually happened. Anyway it's not every day you can spend a tenner and have so much fun; not in Telford anyway, unless you're honing your driving skills in the West Mercian Police Force.

Two guys went down to meet and greet us, then I met Dick, who was going to be my guide. I tried to pinpoint his accent, was it Sheffield, or a little nearer to 'Donny' perhaps? "I'm from California" he said. "Christ,

I'm impressed Dick, you must have started out even earlier than me, this morning." He told me he'd 'popped over' about six years ago to have a look at a couple of caves. Obviously he'd stayed on, to look at a few more.

He went down first, then I readied myself to join him. The bosun's chair returned, I sat in, legs pulled in, arms folded. "Are you ok for a fast descent?" I said I'd practised at the 'Woolly Sheep' by falling down the stairs on Sunday evening. The winchman's helper said that was ideal training; this was going to be much the same, but about 330 feet further. He waved to his colleague and smiled at me. I smiled back, then planet Earth disappeared.

The chair descended quicker than I thought, at first very close to the wall of the chamber.

I was beginning to enjoy the whole experience, when the occasional ice-cold drops of water became more frequent, then suddenly I was falling through a raging, freezing torrent. I was wearing a weather-proof hood and coat and my helmet, but my trousers were only railway denims. I caught my breath, as I lost all feeling between my waist and my padded walking boots. People who know me well say I've never had much sense in that area, anyhow.

I only thought about the cold for a moment, then I was swinging out into the centre of the chamber, open-mouthed as the colours and rock strata flew past me, marvelling at the wonderful kaleidoscope, when too soon, I was on the floor of the cave.

Apart from the two winchmen who met me, Dick and I were the only people down there.

I stepped out onto the surface of the floor; it was moving, they were giant, wet pebbles. Dick said there was a layer of them about sixty feet deep. It was like trying to stand up on slippery semolina pudding, with very hard lumps, like they used to serve in school dinners.

It took me a little while to gain my equilibrium, then I followed Dick's small beam of light across the vast expanse of the cavern. He shone the light around and above me. I began to understand how truly monumental this place really was. The scale was breathtaking. I couldn't see the whole room, but it seemed to extend forever, in every direction.

We walked around together, me always following the light. The underfoot character was different in areas of the cave: first pebbles, then a running river, now a sea of mud, and now dunes like the Sahara Desert.

His light picked out an escape route, high up on one of the walls, explaining this could be used, should the pit become flooded. Not today, thank the Lord.

Steadier on my feet now, I looked up for the first time and saw the bosun's chair singing its way down the winch rope, like a spider on a web, appearing magically from the pinpoint of light far above. Also, the two rivulets gushing into the chamber, the Rathole and the Mousehole, the two rodents who soaked me on the way down. Dick told me the river that formed, disappeared through the pebbles and eventually reached the outside world through Ingleborough Cave.

At one point, whilst we were still alone, he turned off the lamp to conserve the power. He continued his story about the Gill and its adherents, but although I could feel his breath on my face, I couldn't see him. I wasn't in the dark, I was wearing it; wrapped in it like a cocoon; it was part of me.

I am glad to have had that one small, dark, primeval moment. It was the most extraordinary, humbling experience. It brought my life, my place on the earth, and my tenure in it, into crystal clear perspective. In the timeless space of Gaping Gill, out of that total darkness, came one mystical flash of blinding light.

CHAPTER THIRTY ONE

Shap Fell, A Journey

The sun wakes up, and blinks towards the dawning
Of an early, mellow yellow, Autumn
Grey-walled, inner-city, northern morning.
Dwarfed, like scurrying ants we crawl
Between the gaudy trappings of the twentieth century,
Here in dusty, towering, history slumbering,
Red-brick, lumbering, musty mouldering,
Manchester Victoria.
There are railway maps on painted tiles,
That tell the story of the Lancashire and Yorkshire,
And brass-rubbed homage to the company fallen;
Whilst through the sun's shaft shadows
Drops curtain-like, a lingering smell of smoke,
A flag of honours, in this cathedral to the age of steam.
Once proclaiming power, wealth and grandeur,
Now just a memory of faded, jaded splendour.
It's engraved in the very bricks and mortar;
Part of the station's now a parking site for cars,
God knows we're halfway to 'Sic transit gloria'.

To Salford, passing twixt the factories and mills,
No longer dark, and not at all satanic,
Havens of peace and quietness now,
Mews and apartments, luxury high rise flats:
Only the agents and their sale-board hoardings
Show any vestige of industrial panic.

Under the West Coat main line wires
The tempo's rising. The train picks up her feet
The snug carriages are warming.
Beads of moisture forming on the windows,
Sunbathe in new, and unexpected heat.

Put down the stopwatch, set aside the note-pad,
The crackling tannoy brings a message
With a smile; The bar is open.
A carrier bag escorts its swaying owner
Down the swaying aisle,
Two pints of Everard's 'Tiger', and two Jennings best, 'Titanic'.

Framed half-way up the verdant, rock strewn
Northern fells, are woolly, black faced sheep.
In their air-conditioned, mezzanine mountain chapel,
Some are praying,
Some just standing, fast asleep;
So it seems, but this is godless work,
Ovine heads are bent towards survival,
Not evangelical revival.
There's cud chewing to be done,
It's as needful in the sun
As it was last night, under the watery moon.
In the valley down below,
Just like toothpaste on a brush,
The 'Duchess' slides in misty, steamy,
Billowing, pure white hush;
Down the awe-inspiring, timeless, winding,
Breathless, memory binding, Gorge of Lune.

On we thunder, down to Tebay;
Pistons hammering, motion ringing, 'safeties' lifting,
Wheels singing, You can't buy this thrill on E-bay.
Ghostly 'bankers' stand beside the spectral shed,
Traces of cracked and broken bricks,
And ever present buddleia mix,
To give the only clues of earlier, frantic,
Whistle blowing, to and fro-ing, coming, going,
Action; now just history's song, sung by
The northern wind.
Tea cups simmer, through the windows

Steel rails glimmer.
All the quarter-lights are open, hush descends
Upon the carriage, as excited conversation ebbs away:
Machine and man, are once again
About to strain their sinews, pit their wits
Against this hill,
On yet another hero's gladiatorial day.

Shap! For just a moment all the train is floating;
Then Cumbrian solitude erupts in Stanier fury.
The fireman bends to do his work,
And the driver must forget the sounds of protest,
From groaning plates, and screaming metals clamour.
This is Faust before damnation, four cylinder
Rejuvenation; eyes are brighter, back flows vigour,
Old men's faces are becoming new once more.
The ageing process becomes static,
Dorian Gray lives in our attics,
Emotions put on trial, and just like all
Those growing, knowing, times before,
We've found the case is proven, for this four mile bank,
And never ever been in need of any jury.

Past Scout Green and the camera's patron Saint,
St. Kodak, and his massed, stern-faced tutorial;
Climbing high above Shap Wells
And it's quiet, grey-sky pointing, obelisk memorial.
Exhaust beats and pick-axe blows
Have echoed through the summers and the snows,
As the navvies and the railwaymen,
Although in different clothes
Carved their way in blood and sweat,
Music, fighting, beer and mirth,
Through this granite barrier to Penrith,
The Lakeland, Carlisle, and the Solway Firth.

At last, the engine breasts the summit, roll the drum:
Paeans of triumph and thanksgiving
From the dead and from the living,
Today the hours of past and present, both are one.
There's no future, there's no history,
Life itself is timeless mystery,
The old men in sepia photographs
Are still their father's sons.
They'll never disappear, they made us all,
For like the 'Duchess', and her wondrous
Ethereal steam tiara,
Surely, trailing clouds of glory do they come.

Steam in 21st Century. A 'Duchess' on Shap Fell

THE AUTHOR

Bruce Neath was born in Bromsgrove, Worcestershire in 1944.

His ancestors were Welsh.
They were coarse but courteous,
Poetic and romantic, and they worked bloody hard.
The roundelay of early life was Latin grammar, Shakespeare,
the hay wain and the Fordson tractor.
In the family pub they drank and fought,
laughed and wept, and sang like angels.
So they thought.
Refugees from the coal-cleared valleys,
they became entwined with the people of Worcestershire.
Sometimes against their will!
This is the bone structure making the man.
Bruce continues to honour the debt to his past,
and with a temperament of soft linen,
petrol and matches, attempts to keep
the family myth ablaze.
His friends say he has never grown up:
he is eternally glad that they are right.

Breinigsville, PA USA
12 November 2009
227449BV00001B/22/P